ALSO BY DAN BONGINO

Spygate: The Attempted Sabotage of Donald J. Trump

Exonerated: The Failed Takedown of President Trump by the Swamp

FOLLOW
the MONEY

THE SHOCKING DEEP STATE CONNECTIONS
OF THE ANTI-TRUMP CABAL

DAN BONGINO

NEW YORK TIMES BESTSELLING AUTHOR OF
SPYGATE AND *EXONERATED*

A POST HILL PRESS BOOK

Follow the Money:
The Shocking Deep State Connections of the Anti-Trump Cabal
© 2020 by Dan Bongino
All Rights Reserved

ISBN: 978-1-64293-659-9
ISBN (eBook): 978-1-64293-660-5

Cover art by Cody Corcoran

Post Hill Press
New York • Nashville
posthillpress.com

Published in the United States of America

3 4 5 6 7 8 9 10

CONTENTS

CHAPTER 1

Insane in Ukraine

'm going to start in the two places I ended my last book: Ukraine and Washington, DC.

Those are the locations where a group I call the Scandal Manufacturers of America (SMA) sources its best material.

The SMA is the unofficial coalition of crybaby Democrats, holier-than-thou liberal media pundits, and delusional Never-Trumpers who have dedicated themselves to the takedown of the elected president of the United States, Donald J. Trump.

I've already devoted two books to documenting and dismantling the SMA's work. The first, *Spygate*, revealed how this group manufactured a bogus Russia-collusion story, which, fortunately, failed to stop or discredit the election of Trump. The second, *Exonerated*, documented the plug-and-play efforts by Clinton operatives and senior law enforcement officials in the FBI and the Department of Justice to remove Trump from office by fabricating and laundering misleading "evidence" of a supposed conspiracy. As the world now knows, special prosecutor Robert Mueller's mission to uncover that "evidence" was an utter failure. For the record, much of that second book's assertions about FBI and special investigator chicanery have been proven correct in a report issued by the Department

1

of Justice's Inspector General Michael Horowitz. That report concluded that applications used to obtain warrants used by the FBI to spy on Trump campaign advisor Carter Page contained seventeen major errors and omissions.[1]

As for the infamous "Steele dossier," the collection of fabrications, rumors, and lies about the Trump campaign, Horowitz concluded, "the FBI failed to reassess the Steele reporting relied upon in the FISA [Foreign Intelligence Surveillance Act] applications, and did not fully advise the [National Security Division] or [Office of Intelligence]. We also found that the FBI did not aggressively seek to obtain certain potentially important information from Steele."[2]

Undaunted by two elaborate failures, the shameless Scandal Manufacturers of America pivoted to a new chapter in its senseless saga. Just months after the pointless Mueller probe came to an end, they decided to waste thousands of man-hours paralyzing Capitol Hill by launching impeachment proceedings to remove the president. As everyone knows, Ukraine was at the center of that effort.

Or should I say, *failed* effort?

I'll get into the absurdity of the impeachment case mounted against the president, but let's zoom in on Ukraine. Why is this nation so important? Why is it a magnet for trouble? Why should a few sentences from the president of the United States to his counterpart in Kyiv, Volodymyr Zelensky, detonate hand-wringing, sky-is-falling statements about the collapse of our republic?

Trump was doing what presidents do. But here are some quotes from the Ukraine experts trotted out by Adam Schiff's House Intelligence Committee to expose the so-called heinous behavior of the president. Let's see if these excerpts fully explain this Eastern European enigma.

> Ukraine is a battleground for great power competition, with a hot war for the control of territory and a hybrid war to control Ukraine's leadership. —FORMER AMBASSADOR TO UKRAINE MARIE YOVANOVITCH[3]

Ukraine is a genuine and vibrant democracy and an example to other post-Soviet countries and beyond—from Moscow to Hong Kong. —DAVID HOLMES, COUNSELOR FOR POLITICAL AFFAIRS, U.S. EMBASSY, UKRAINE[4]

Ukraine is a valued partner of the United States, and it plays an important role in our national security. —FIONA HILL, SENIOR DIRECTOR FOR EUROPEAN AND RUSSIAN AFFAIRS, NATIONAL SECURITY COUNCIL[5]

Ukraine is making progress. —LIEUTENANT COLONEL ALEXANDER VINDMAN, DIRECTOR FOR EUROPEAN AFFAIRS, NATIONAL SECURITY COUNCIL[6]

The most accurate and honest description of Ukraine that I heard during the hearings didn't actually come from the hearings. It came from a *Seinfeld* episode that someone emailed me. You don't have to be a fan of that particular sitcom to appreciate the prophetic political analysis that aired on January 19, 1995. In the key scene, Kramer, the show's tall, gangly hipster, is playing the board game Risk on the subway—a funny image in and of itself—and he's taunting his opponent. "You know what Ukraine is?" he laughs. "It's a sitting duck. It's a road-apple."

At least that is in the ballpark. Ukraine is a lot of things, obviously. It's a country populated by wonderful, hard-working people who are desperate for honest leadership. Yet, the Ukrainians have been consistently let down by a broken political class eager for power and riches, and lacking in the one trait that could turn the political tide: morality. The experts on the Hill weren't actually wrong with their passing summaries. But they weren't right, either. They didn't tell the whole picture. As we dig deeper and deeper into the story and unravel the corrupt connections surrounding this chaotic country, no description may be more accurate than the one the creatures of the DC swamp should have offered under oath:

> Ukraine is a giant, twenty-four-hour ATM. A broken slot machine
> that spewed out money to greedy politicos, lobbyists, and, yes, a son
> of the vice president of the United States.

That would have been accurate. Maybe not so much right now, when everyone is on their best behavior with the spotlight on Kyiv. But understanding the vast, money-printing, influence-peddling, backstabbing, dog-eat-dog corruption of Ukraine would have helped the world understand why Donald Trump was having the conversation that set off the entire, absurd, impeachment charade.

Ukraine was an influence-peddling paradise. It was vital to Russian interests.

It was vital to American interests.

And that made it vital to anyone with self-interests in generating cash.

By now, Hunter Biden, the son of former vice president and current presidential candidate Joe Biden, is the most famous of these human handout homing devices. But there were many swamp rats—from both sides of the aisle—who swooped into Kyiv to make mega-withdrawals. I've documented a bunch of this, but we now know far more about the players and the sinister connections many of them shared.

Let's start with the man who is really ground zero for all the manufactured Trump scandals: Paul Manafort.

Seriously. I'm not here to defend Manafort. He brought damaging baggage with him to the Trump campaign—serving first as a consultant and then the campaign chairman—and it cast a toxic shadow over the candidate's entire organization. Collusion hoaxers were all too happy to leverage Manafort's shady dealings for political gain. In *Exonerated,* I explained how and why Manafort's presence raised huge flags for Fusion GPS, the company hired by Hillary Clinton's campaign to conduct "opposition research"—his links to Putin's pals, billionaire Oleg Deripaska, and former Ukrainian president Viktor Yanukovych were suspect.

Now Fusion GPS's Glenn Simpson has confirmed all this in his own book, which came out two months *after* my book, noting the very same *Wall Street Journal* articles that I cited—imagine that!—and revealing he'd been tracking Manafort for years:

> To Fusion, Manafort wasn't just another Beltway bandit from yesteryear. He was a seminal figure in the annals of Washington consulting, a famously avaricious and venal operative.... Here was a consultant who had a history of blending foreign lobbying with his work on presidential campaigns, and, more recently, had spent more than a decade working actively against U.S. interests in Europe....[7]

Manafort lasted about six months with the Trump campaign. While Simpson and his operatives were scouring for dirt, Democratic National Committee consultant Alexandra Chalupa was also ringing alarm bells, telling anyone she could that Manafort was linked to Ukraine's personal Putin puppet president Yanukovych and his corrupt administration—which had been overthrown in a popular uprising. But what brought Manafort down was a report in the *New York Times* about a mysterious black ledger.

"Handwritten ledgers show $12.7 million in undisclosed cash payments designated for Mr. Manafort from Mr. Yanukovych's pro-Russian political party from 2007 to 2012, according to Ukraine's newly formed National Anti-Corruption Bureau," the *Times* reported.[8]

The Ukraine anti-corruption cops were also examining offshore companies that may have been used to funnel cash to Yanukovych's cronies and hundreds of "murky" transactions, including an "$18 million deal to sell Ukrainian cable television assets to a partnership put together by Mr. Manafort" and his old Russian billionaire client Oleg Deripaska.[9]

The allegations of possible wrong-doing involving Russian and Ukrainian oligarchs, combined with a dip in polling numbers for the Trump campaign, forced Manafort to resign just five days after the black ledger report.

Here's the thing: the initial reports of the black ledger strained credibility from day one. This giant, incriminating piece of evidence initially surfaced out of nowhere, just as Paul Manafort joined Team Trump. Ukrainian Parliament member Sergii Leshchenko said he received twenty-two pages of mysterious financial transactions in his mailbox in February 2016. Three months later, Viktor Trepak, former deputy head of the Security Service of Ukraine, revealed the ledger had been left on his doorstep, abandoned like a helpless orphan! It was eight hundred pages long and documented shocking transactions from 2007 to 2012.[10]

Why would the thing exist at all? Unless Ukraine gives tax deductions for illegal payouts, why leave a paper trail? Leshchenko offered up this explanation: "Perhaps the idea was that a paper document was safer because it can't be stolen by hacking into the computer and law enforcement officers won't find it if they seize equipment during a search."[11]

Okay. That's possible. These guys aren't all rocket scientists. And to be totally honest, the idea that someone would fabricate eight hundred pages is a little nuts when a hundred pages would suffice. But if Leshchenko's explanation is plausible, is it also within the bounds of reason that someone with scores to settle fabricated the document, too, and then circulated it? The provenance of the document has never been established. In terms of being verifiable, there is a legitimate argument that it's as "real" as the Loch Ness Monster.

Manafort's business partner Rick Gates, who was also a member of the Trump campaign team, told FBI agents and prosecutors from Special Counsel Robert Mueller's team that the black ledger was a fake. Gates had no reason to lie; he became a cooperating witness for the hapless Mueller team and eventually copped a plea deal.

"The ledger was completely made up," Gates said in a written summary of an April 2018 special counsel's interview, according to reporter John Solomon.[12]

Gates then confirmed the veracity of the summary, telling Solomon, "The black ledger was a fabrication. It was never real, and this fact has since been proven true." As for the *New York Times* story that set the black ledger narrative in motion? "The article was completely false," he told Mueller's team. "As you now know, there were no cash payments. The payments were wired. The ledger was completely made up."

Gates also claimed the ledger didn't fit with how Yanukovych's party kept records. And if it did fit, it still should never have surfaced. "All the real records were burned when the party headquarters was set on fire when Yanukovych fled the country," Gates told the investigators, according to the interview summary.[13]

So, what was the point of the black ledger? Who benefited from its existence? The fact is, if the transactions in the ledger were true, they exposed Manafort's failure to declare enormous sums of income, exposing him to potential money laundering charges. They also offered proof that Manafort had failed to register as a foreign agent working for Ukraine—although prosecuting anyone for violating the Foreign Agents Registration Act was practically unheard of before the Spygate scandal broke.[14] Seen in this light, the answer to the question of who benefited from the black ledger is: anyone who wanted to blow the whistle on Manafort's legal problems.

That begs the question, who would want to see Donald Trump's campaign chairman get in big trouble? Obviously, Trump's opponents at this time were the likely suspects: Hillary Clinton, the Democratic National Committee, and a legion of Obama and Clinton loyalists who would be out of office and out of power if a Republican were to sit in the Oval Office.

In other words, hurting Trump's campaign chief would unquestionably hurt Trump. But let's cast a wider net. Damaging Trump wasn't the original goal of the Scandal Manufacturers of America. Stopping him was. So, getting the goods on Paul Manafort was ideal for a prosecutor looking to collect damning testimony. And if you were a political operative looking to ruin an election campaign or cripple a presidency, cataloguing Manafort's misdeeds was just what you needed.

For prosecutors and biased FBI agents hunting down evidence of Trump-campaign collusion with Russia, the black ledger was a dream come true. It created legal leverage to exert on Paul Manafort, the guy running the campaign, and Rick Gates, who was not only Manafort's business partner but also served as the deputy campaign chairman.

If there was collusion, these would be the guys investigators would want to talk to. And the ledger provided a way to force Manafort and Gates to cooperate with the Trump-obsessed prosecutors and tell investigators everything they wanted to know.

Gates became a cooperating witness, pleading guilty to charges of conspiring to defraud the United States of millions he earned working for a political party in Ukraine and of lying to the FBI during an interview.[15] In terms of delivering evidence of collusion, Gates, despite his plea bargain deal, provided the Mueller witch hunters with zero damning evidence tying the president to collusion. The closest he came to any untoward Moscow mixing was a revelation that Manafort had Gates provide Konstantin Kilimnik—an employee of Deripaska—with meaningless campaign polling updates. Yes, the FBI believed Kilimnik had ties to Russian intelligence, but it is also worth noting he was once a source for the Obama-era State Department. Here's the Mueller Report's own "blockbuster" work:

> Manafort instructed Rick Gates, his deputy on the Campaign and a longtime employee, to provide Kilimnik with updates on the Trump Campaign—including internal polling data, although Manafort claims not to recall that specific instruction. Manafort expected Kilimnik to share that information with others in Ukraine and with Deripaska. Gates periodically sent such polling data to Kilimnik during the campaign.[16]

Again, Manafort is no hero. He told Gates that steering information to Deripaska, who had reportedly launched a number of lawsuits against Manafort for missing funds, might help the campaign chair resolve his disputes with the powerful Russian oligarch. But Mueller clearly gave both Gates and Manafort a pass on this issue—here's the report's discussion of the polling data:

> ...the Office could not assess what Kilimnik (or others he may have given it to) did with it. The Office did not identify evidence of a connection between Manafort's sharing polling data and Russia's interference in the election, which had already been reported by U.S. media outlets at the time of the August 2 meeting. The investigation did not establish that Manafort otherwise coordinated with the Russian government on its election-interference efforts.[17]

All this leads me to two points.

The first is that whatever the questionable black ledger revealed, it had nothing to do with Spygate and Russiagate. It was what mystery and movie writers call a "MacGuffin"—the issue, question, or event that sets a whole plot in motion. It's the titular bird in *The Maltese Falcon*—the statue that every character covets. It's the search for the missing future groom Doug in bachelor-party-gone-wrong movie *The Hangover*. It's the mystery behind the meaning of the "Rosebud," the last word the protagonist utters before dying in the classic film *Citizen Kane*. The black ledger drove the collusion narrative. Manafort was a target as soon as he joined the Trump team, as I've previously documented. But the ledger cast a dark cloud of suspicion over Paul Manafort and the campaign, and it provided a way to disparage Trump and investigate Manafort and Team Trump. And yet, what did it prove besides Manafort's financial chicanery? Nothing. But it was just what investigators needed to begin working on their failed takedown.

The second point is that the FBI and Mueller prosecutors used the information in the ledger to probe Manafort and create a blizzard of negative press reports about a top Trump associate. They followed his money, from Ukraine to shell companies and hidden bank accounts in Cyprus, Seychelles, and the Caribbean nation Saint Vincent and the Grenadines to the U.S.[18] Manafort and Gates weren't the only ones abusing the 24/7/365 money machine that was Ukraine. They were far from the only Americans with suspicious connections to corrupt officials with ties to both Moscow and Washington. And, as I'm going to reveal, others who were ready to dive into the cash-rich political world of Kyiv had plenty of presidential connections.

Not with Trump—but with Obama and Clinton.

And many of these players knew each other. They shared allegiances to previous administrations. Some were colleagues. Some were careerists. Some were craven operatives.

The Scandal Manufacturers of America conveniently ignored the unfortunate optics emanating from these citizens of the swamp and their behavior. But that's over.

It's time to follow their money and connections.

THE SOROS CIRCLE, PART I

Just a month after the black ledger surfaced, other disturbing big money influencing operations were building up steam in the shadows of Ukraine. One of them involved figures who would turn up at the center of the Trump impeachment proceedings, including George Soros, the billionaire Democratic Party underwriter, who has rarely met a liberal cause he didn't like.

Soros has admitted that his foundation fund, at least originally, was formed out of self-interest. "A charitable lead trust is a very interesting tax gimmick," he admitted in a bout of shocking candor. "The idea is that you commit your assets to a trust and you put a certain amount of money into charity every year. And then after you have given the money for however many years, the principal that remains can be left [to one's heirs] without estate or gift tax. So this was the way I set up the trust for my children." Soros reportedly began by planning to donate up to $3 million a year for twenty years.[19] Since then, he has given away many multiples of that contribution plan by launching Open Society and providing it with $32 billion, while also donating at least $75 million to various political candidates.[20]

One of the places he donated to, at least indirectly, was Ukraine. In 2017, Soros gave $1 million to the Democracy Integrity Project (TDIP), a group founded by Daniel J. Jones to supposedly investigate interference in Western elections by hostile foreign powers. Jones, a former FBI analyst and staffer for Sen. Dianne Feinstein (D-CA), wrangled over $7 million in revenue for his nonprofit, according to tax filings. His group then paid $3,323,924 for "research consulting" to Bean LLC—the parent company of Fusion GPS.[21]

But let's reverse engineer this: Jones, it turns out, didn't just hire the firm that kicked off the entire Spygate fiasco; *Fusion GPS hired itself.* Here, verbatim, is Glenn Simpson describing—in the third person— how The Democracy Integrity Project (TDIP) was born after Simpson reached out to Jones:

> The two met in the conference room of Jones's downtown office on the Sunday after the inauguration period. Simpson told Jones the whole story from Fusion's initial assignment, in 2015, to the events of the final days of the campaign. Jones had worked on various Russia-related security issues at the Intelligence Committee. He agreed that the United States was as unprepared to counter the new Russian security threat as it had been to cope with al-Qaeda 15 years before. Simpson raised the idea of setting up a new group that could work with Fusion and other investigators around the world to expose Russian subversion operations in the United States and other western democracies. Jones said he thought it needed to be done—right away.[22]

Okay. So, George Soros, who in 2015 gave $16 million to groups supporting Hillary Clinton, also gave $1 million to a group conceived of by Glenn Simpson. Then, Simpson's company, Fusion GPS, which initiated Spygate, was paid more than $3 million—almost half TDIP's budget—to research how the Russian intelligence operations were influencing elections around the globe. I have no doubt Russian intelligence is trying to influence elections. The U.S. does it. China does it. That is what superpowers do. But Glenn Simpson, who obviously couldn't figure out the difference between national interest and self-interest, was not the guy to spearhead this project. There is a preponderance of evidence that suggests he was a profiteering partisan hack.

Curiously, Soros wasn't the only Clintonista to surface in the TDIP story. When Simpson and Jones appealed to the tech community, John Podesta—the former chief of staff for Bill Clinton and the chairman of Hillary Clinton's presidential campaign—was "one of the most helpful," according to Simpson.

Are you dizzy yet?

Stay with me.

Podesta's involvement is interesting for a couple of reasons. First, his personal Gmail account was compromised in a basic phishing attack that has been attributed to Russian hacking. Both Podesta and the DNC's emails were widely released on Wikileaks, leading to a number of huge embarrassments for the campaign Podesta ran. Among the revelations: interim DNC chair Donna Brazile obtained debate questions ahead of time for Hillary Clinton; the party was discussing creating liberal Catholic groups as part of its get-out-the-vote campaign, a potentially explosive covert campaign operation; and senior campaign leaders stated that supposed ally Saudi Arabia was backing ISIS's war against the West. Never mind the irony of the man who suffered the most basic of online attacks making introductions to big tech firms; it is clear Podesta had a vested interest in Simpson's project. It's not at all clear that the email interference helped Trump beat toxic Hillary, but nobody had a bigger revenge motive against Russian operatives than Podesta—unless you count Clinton.

The second curious thing is that John Podesta's brother, Tony Podesta, was under investigation for cashing in on the Ukraine money train. As chairman of the Podesta Group, Tony was one of the biggest lobbying forces in the backwater known as Washington, DC. Although he worked both sides of the aisle, in 2016 he ponied up or raised nearly

$900,000 in donations to Clinton and the Democratic Party.[23] In 2018, investigators probed the Podesta Group chairman for his ties to Paul Manafort and for possible violations of the Foreign Agents Registration Act. From 2012 to 2014, Podesta was paid at least $1.2 million to promote a Ukraine campaign conceived by Manafort and Gates, and backed by Viktor Yanukovych, the deposed pro-Russian Ukrainian president, and the Party of Regions.

About five years after cashing those checks, the Podesta Group filed with the FARA Registration Unit, claiming it had previously been told by the European Centre for Modern Ukraine that it was not "directly or indirectly supervised, directed, controlled, financed or supervised" by a foreign government or political party.[24]

Tony Podesta resigned from his post as this story broke. In September 2019, investigators closed the investigation without pressing charges. Former Obama White House counsel Greg Craig, however, was indicted for lying to the Justice Department and concealing information about work he did on the same project. Craig beat the charges, but all of this speaks to the larger point: Ukraine was a fountain of funding for the denizens of the swamp, many of whom worked together on many different levels.[25]

And few are woven as complexly as Soros.

THE SOROS CIRCLE, PART II

In 1990, Soros's Open Society Foundation created the International Renaissance Foundation (IRF) in Ukraine to help foster the former Eastern Bloc country's transition to democracy and a market economy. Four years later, the Open Society was pouring in $14 million a year for the IRF to distribute to various projects in Ukraine. Thirty years later, the IRF was still receiving nearly $8 million in funds from Soros's group. In 2014, the IRF "and its grantees were active supporters" in the creation of the Anti-Corruption Centre of Ukraine (AntAC).[26]

AntAC, which received $289,285—that's 17 percent of its total annual funding through the end of 2018—from Soros's group,[27] was started when rampant corruption was plaguing Ukraine. It was instrumental in the creation of the National Anticorruption Bureau of Ukraine (NABU)—a new, independent, government law-enforcement agency, separate from the prosecutor general's office—to handle the biggest corruption cases. NABU was set up with funding from Western governments. The Federal Bureau of Investigation also provided support.

In February 2015, Viktor Shokin was appointed the prosecutor general of Ukraine. As I reported in *Exonerated*, he quickly came under fire for helping the owner of energy company Burisma Holdings, Mykola Zlochevsky, regain control of $23 million that had been frozen by UK authorities. Zlochevsky, who famously struck a deal appointing Hunter Biden, the train-wreck son of then-Vice President Joe Biden, to Burisma's Board of Directors in May 2014, had been the ecology minister under former Putin pal Yanukovych.

Shokin later told investigative reporter John Solomon he had begun to initiate a Burisma probe. This "included interrogations and other crime-investigation procedures into all members of the executive board, including Hunter Biden."

Shokin did not get to question anyone, however, because Joe Biden, the vice president of the United States at the time, threatened to withhold a $1 billion loan to Ukraine unless Shokin was removed. According to bragging Biden's own videotaped account, he attended a meeting with Ukrainian president Poroshenko and then-Prime Minister Yatsenyuk and said, "'I'm leaving in six hours. If the prosecutor is not fired, you're not getting the money.' Well, son of a bitch. He got fired. And they put in place someone who was solid at the time."[28]

Interestingly, nobody accused Biden of an illicit quid pro quo when he proudly told the story at an event for the Council on Foreign Relations in early 2018. But even more interesting is that by targeting Shokin for removal, Biden was pushing out a man on record as saying he was going to investigate Burisma and interview his son Hunter. I blew the whistle on Biden's incredibly suspect behavior in *Exonerated*, but it can't be overstated just how inappropriate his actions were. Biden responded by claiming Shokin was corrupt, as have some other Shokin critics, and that may or may not be accurate. But what is absolutely undeniable is that Biden was forcing a foreign government—our *ally*—to conduct itself in a certain way (by firing the prosecutor looking into the company his son was working for) or lose access to a massive financial aid package in the form of a loan.

Fast-forward to May 2020 and the extent to which the removal of Shokin was a quid pro quo deal, engineered by Biden, became even more clear than it was before and more shocking in Biden's brazen "my-way-or-the-highway" behavior.

On May 19, 2020, Ukrainian lawmaker Andriy Derkach released tapes of alleged calls between Biden and Ukrainian president Poroshenko. In one call, Poroshenko admits doing Biden's dirty work. In another, Biden states that he is releasing a $1 billion loan because Shokin was bounced.

"Despite the fact that (Shokin) didn't have any corruption charges, we don't have any information about him doing something wrong, I especially asked him…to resign," Poroshenko told Biden in a recording from February 18, 2016.[29]

In another recording—apparently made on March 22, 2016, the date the White House issued a press release confirming the two leaders talked[30]—Biden and Poroshenko discussed who could be appointed prosecutor general, and the eventual replacement, Yuriy Lutsenko, was mentioned. Poroshenko even offered to find another candidate if Biden wanted.[31]

After the deal was done, Biden made explicit he would deliver the quid for Poroshenko's quo: "I'm a man of my word. And now that the new prosecutor general is in place, we're ready to move forward to signing that new $1 billion loan guarantee."[32]

Can Biden's inappropriate actions—for his son's personal gains—get ANY clearer?

And yet the mainstream media continues to act like Biden's behavior is perfectly acceptable, swallowing Biden camp dismissals wholesale.

Ladies and gentlemen, Joe Biden committed a quid pro quo deal in full daylight and admitted it. He is the true Teflon politician. If this won't stick, what will?

In 2016, as the U.S. presidential election heated up, Ukraine's prosecutor general's office began an investigation into AntAC (which was heavily funded by Soros) about the possible misuse of $2.2 million of funds and had an inquiry sent to then-U.S. Ambassador Geoffrey Pyatt. George Kent, the chargé d'affaires—that's diplomatic-speak for the second-in-command at an embassy—responded to Deputy Prosecutor General Yuriy Stolyarchuk with a two-page letter that said the United States had "no concerns about the use of our assistance funds" and noted "we have accounted for every single foreign assistance dollar" spent on projects in Ukraine. Deep into the letter, however, Kent then pressured Stolyarchuk about AntAC.

"The investigation into the Anti-Corruption Action Center, based on the assistance they have received from us, is similarly misplaced," Kent wrote on April 4, 2016,[33] less than a week after Shokin was removed from office. So, at the time, the letter arrived with a void at Ukraine's top legal office as no replacement had been named. Kent was obviously applying pressure to the agency over Soros's pet project.

This pressure from American diplomats didn't stop, according to Yuri Lutsenko, Shokin's replacement. The new prosecutor general attended a meeting with the new U.S. ambassador to Ukraine, Marie Yovanovitch, and said he was shocked when she "gave me a list of people whom we should not prosecute." He claimed the list included a founder of AntAC and two members of Parliament who supported the group, according to a John Solomon report.[34]

The U.S. Embassy in Kyiv called Shokin's charge a fabrication. But Solomon has reported that numerous Ukrainian sources confirmed there was American pressure to back off AntAC. The message to Ukraine officials, Solomon relayed, was "Don't target AntAC in the middle of an American presidential election in which Soros was backing Hillary Clinton to succeed another Soros favorite, Barack Obama."[35]

Or as another top Ukrainian official put it: "We ran right into a buzzsaw and we got bloodied."[36]

Lutsenko, the former minister of interior affairs of Ukraine, said he thought American embassy bigwigs didn't want to call attention to Ukrainian anti-corruption measures. "At the time, Ms. Ambassador thought our interviews of the Ukrainian citizens, of the Ukrainian civil servants who were frequent visitors in the U.S. Embassy could cast a shadow on that anti-corruption policy," he said.[37]

Why would Chargé d'Affaires George Kent and Ambassador Yovanovitch try to influence the investigations occurring in a sovereign country? To answer that question, it helps to remember the probe was focused on an organization that had the backing of the Obama administration, the State Department, some in the FBI, and a certain billionaire private citizen who has injected himself into U.S. and global politics at an almost unprecedented level. Nobody wanted an investigation because it might expose sinister connections that defy coincidence and destroy a false liberal narrative that they are the movement looking to defeat and expose monied influences in politics.

This becomes clear in light of the memos Solomon uncovered from Soros's Open Society Foundations advocating U.S. involvement in Ukraine and offering "behind the scenes advice and support to Ukrainian partner Anti-Corruption Action Centre's efforts to generate corruption litigation in Europe and the U.S. respecting state assets stolen by senior Ukrainian leaders."

Solomon reported the memo contained a chart of Ukrainians to be investigated, "including some with ties to Manafort."[38] Although he doesn't name names, it is highly likely that the memo mentioned Dmitry Firtash, a Ukrainian billionaire. Soros has energy interests in Europe, as does Firtash. And there is little doubt the men are rivals.[39] But in 2015, a year before all this drama, Firtash beat civil charges asserting he had engaged in money laundering with Manafort.

Remember, all this pressure on Ukrainian prosecutors was happening in the spring of 2016 just when Paul Manafort had joined Team Trump and the underdog candidate was shocking the world by trouncing all-comers in the Republican primaries to become the presumptive nominee. Also at this time, Glenn Simpson was padding his bank account while conducting "opposition research" on Trump and setting up his hit on Manafort. Meanwhile, Alexandra Chalupa, the DNC Ukraine expert, was yapping to anyone who would listen about Manafort's dirty money connections. And now, it turns out that a foundation owned by Soros, the biggest liberal donor in the universe, was interested in probing Manafort's other Ukraine associates and was actually funding the perfect vehicle to do that: AntAC.

Is anyone surprised that the U.S. embassy wanted to stop inquiries that might look into and derail AntAC's work? Especially if that organization might "uncover" more dirt to kick on the Trump campaign chairman—and if that dirt-digging operation was backed by a man who was giving Hillary Clinton millions of dollars for her failed campaign?

The connections are staggering.

They make you think Ukraine isn't the only country with a corruption problem.

THE SOROS CIRCLE, PART III

AntAC wasn't the only Soros-funded group to target Firtash. In 2018, the Open Society–backed Campaign Legal Center filed a complaint with the Federal Election Commission charging that a Russian-speaking Ukrainian businessman named Igor Fruman and a Russian-born businessman named Lev Parnas created Global Energy Producers, LLC as a shell corporation to anonymously funnel $325,000 to a pro-Trump super PAC.[40]

This kicked off an investigation into Parnas and Fruman which uncovered a $1 million payment to Parnas' wife from Firtash's lawyer. I don't want to spend too much time on this. But again, here we have Ukraine big shots with millions of dollars engaging in corrupt behavior, and others vying for influence with top American leadership. Duped by Parnas and Fruman's questionable credentials, Firtash may have been under the impression that they had the pull and clout to make his legal hassles vanish. Instead, the donation-happy duo are now being prosecuted.

Infuriatingly, when the head of Burisma does something very similar, like showering absurd amounts of cash on Hunter Biden, the establishment response is "Nothing to see here. Move along."

If AntAC had focused on the Biden fiasco, it might have turned up a newly surfaced document from early 2016 that flagged "suspicious" transactions involving Burisma and voiced concern about the company's ties to the vice president's son. An alarming memo dated February 18, 2016, from a Latvian investigative agency alerted Ukraine's financial authorities to a probe.

"The Office for Prevention of Laundering of Proceeds Derived from Criminal Activity…is currently investigating suspicious activity of Burisma Holdings Limited," read the notice from the Latvian watchdog agency. As John Solomon reported:

> The Latvian law enforcement memo identified a series of loan payments totaling about $16.6 million that were routed from companies in Belize and the United Kingdom to Burisma through Ukraine's PrivatBank between 2012 and 2015.
>
> The flagged funds were "partially transferred" to Hunter Biden, a board member at Burisma since May 2014, and three other officials working for the Ukrainian natural gas company, the Latvian memo said.[41]

The Latvian inquiry stalled when Ukrainian officials failed to respond.[42] But this just adds to the dark cloud of suspicion and possible malfeasance surrounding the Bidens and their questionable ties to a company engulfed in widespread allegations of corruption. Given that, you'd think that AntAC, the so-called anti-corruption champion, would be interested in probing this relationship. But when your benefactor is an enormous investor in the Democratic Party committed to spending millions to try and stop Trump, maybe that investigation isn't very appealing.

Anyone who thinks Soros isn't fixated on stopping Trump is dreaming. In March 2020, as America was besieged by COVID-19, the lethal coronavirus that started in China and nearly crippled the entire world, Soros's Democracy political action committee donated $3 million to Priorities USA Action, the Democratic Party's super PAC. The money was earmarked to fund a series of ads in four swing states attacking Trump's response to the virus.[43] Amazing. Instead of donating that money to hospitals or struggling workers or small businesses, Soros remained fixated on removing the president. Instead of purchasing respirators and ventilators with his vast wealth, he used the cash to pump out ads insulting Trump. If Soros wants to complain about the spread of the virus in the U.S., he should start with the totalitarian communist country that locked itself down and then foisted the virus on the world by refusing to seal its borders. That country is China, and its ruling party is hell-bent on destabilizing the West. The blame for COVID-19 starts and ends with Beijing, as I explain more fully in Chapter 9 of this book.

Soros's contribution to this ignoble cause was his second donation to Priorities USA Action in 2020. His PAC had given $2 million in January.[44] It is anyone's guess how many more millions he will spend in the run-up to the November election that, as of June 2020, will have him backing quid pro quo Joe Biden, the proud father of handout happy Hunter Biden.

THE WIDENING CIRCLE

There are other characters in the Ukraine story who are worth noting. They orbit between the Obama White House, U.S. law enforcement and intelligence divisions, the world of Soros, and, of course, Ukraine.

FBI agent Karen Greenaway, a veteran money-laundering expert, was sent to Ukraine during the Obama administration to help the Prosecutor General's Office track funds. Senior members of the FBI, as I documented in *Exonerated*, and as Inspector General Michael Horowitz confirmed, have been instrumental in waging a campaign against Trump. But I have every belief the vast majority of agents at the bureau are nonpartisan law enforcement professionals. I have no way of knowing what Agent Greenaway's politics are. But I do know that she recently retired from the bureau and promptly signed on to become a board member of AntAC. Assuming this is a paid position—most board gigs are—Greenaway is now also part of the Soros cabal, whether she likes it or not.

AntAC is run by Daria Kaleniuk, an American-educated lawyer. She has been, as you might expect, an outspoken defender of her organization, noting that "the E.U., the U.S., the governments of the United Kingdom, the Netherlands and the Czech Republic, the Global Fund" have supplied her organization with financial support.[45] And, while that is no doubt true, it doesn't diminish the clout or influence of America's premiere political patron. In fact, AntAC lists its donors on its website in apparent decreasing order:

01. U.S. government
02. EU and Member States governments
03. Private international funds
04. Charitable donations from companies and individuals[46]

This makes it seem that the contribution from Soros's foundation would be the least significant. But that is misleading since we know that it gave millions in previous years, including 2019 when Soros donations accounted for 17 percent of the budget. If the six entities Kaleniuk names gave as much as Soros—6 x 17 percent—well, that would come to 102 percent. And that's without including Soros's donation! All of which is to say that AntAC's efforts to distance itself from Soros should be taken with a mountainous grain of salt.

What is also true—and this is very important—is that, according to White House logs, Kaleniuk visited the White House on December 9, 2015. While there, she reportedly met with Eric Ciaramella, a CIA employee working on the National Security Council. Getting meetings in the White House is no easy thing. You need connections. How did Kaleniuk rate? Who opened those doors for her? Why did she meet with Ciaramella? We don't know exactly. But we do know that Ciaramella was very interested in Ukraine.[47]

Very, very interested.

How do we know this? Forgive me, but I don't want to get too far ahead of the story.

The Obama White House, it turns out, was an unofficial club for Ukraine obsessives. The logs also reveal that Alexandra Chalupa visited the White House twenty-seven times. Was she there on DNC business or her crusade to expose Manafort? Did she meet with the CIA's Ciaramella?

Because as it turns out, the enigmatic CIA operative Ciaramella met with several leading members of the Scandal Manufacturers of America. Keep him in the back of your mind because he will reappear in a very prominent role by the end of this book.

CHAPTER 2

The Trumped-Up Meeting

I want to revisit another so-called Spygate hotspot: Donald Trump Jr.'s office in Trump Tower, where a supposedly sinister meeting took place that "proved" the campaign was working hand-in-glove with Moscow.

This was one of the most ridiculous manufactured "scandals" in all of the unofficial Operation Remove Trump movement—although I have to admit it isn't easy to rank one absurd fabrication against the other. New revelations emerged in 2020—nearly four years after this utter non-event occurred—that demonstrated how and why this innocuous twenty-minute meeting should have been almost immediately dismissed as a non-event.

Instead, it was presented as proof of a collusion convention.

Let's go back to July 8, 2017. That's when the *New York Times* published a signature alarmist article, "Trump Team Met with Lawyer Linked to Kremlin During Campaign." The piece reported that on June 9, 2016, a Trump Tower meeting took place between Russian lawyer Natalia Veselnitskaya and senior members of the Trump campaign, including Donald Trump Jr., Paul Manafort, and Jared Kushner. "This episode," the Gray Lady sensationalists wrote with breathless urgency, "is the first confirmed private meeting between a Russian national and members of Mr. Trump's inner circle during the campaign."[1]

The gist of this, as read by the left-wing media, was: *OMG! This is proof that all those rumors about collusion in the press must be 100 percent true.*

Two days after the piece ran, Rob Goldstone, the publicist who arranged the meeting, told the *Times* that his client, Russian pop star Emin Agalarov, requested the PR man set up the meeting with Donald Trump Jr. and Veselnitskaya. "He said, 'I'm told she has information about illegal campaign contributions to the D.N.C.,'" recalled Goldstone, referring to the Democratic National Committee.[2]

Eventually, other sinister-sounding allegations filtered into the press. Goldstone's email to Trump Jr. leaked, describing Veselnitskaya and her offering—"some official documents and information that would incriminate Hillary and her dealings with Russia"—in breathless terms. "This is obviously very very high level and sensitive information but is part of Russia and its government's support for Mr. Trump." The email response from Donald Trump Jr., who had an understandable interest in opposition research, was portrayed as equally ominous: "If it's what you say, I love it, especially later in the summer." But it was just a campaign leader doing his job.[3]

The Trump team quickly downplayed the meeting, saying nothing of any importance was discussed. By July 11, Goldstone called the meeting "the most inane nonsense l ever heard. And I was actually agitated by it." That same day, Donald Trump Jr. released his entire email chain with Goldstone, revealing that, at most, he thought it might result in some preliminary opposition research.[4] The disavowals and transparency were widely dismissed, and the Trump team participants were roundly attacked on a number of counts. To some critics, it appeared the campaign was looking for dirt on Clinton from a foreign agent. But the fact is, they had no idea what Veselnitskaya had to offer. On another level, how would that have been any different from the Clinton campaign hiring Fusion GPS to have former British spy Christopher Steele dig up dirt on Trump? To others, eager for any sliver of evidence to advance their collusion conspiracy theory, this was evidence of possible "collusion" with Russians. That's a lot of possibles, but not a lot of probables. In the flood of stories about the meeting, reports surfaced of Kushner and Manafort texting about the meeting being a waste of time. But that wasn't good enough to silence the sky-is-falling claims of the liberal media and their hysterical Never-Trump allies.

The facts, now that they have emerged, prove that the meeting was, indeed, a waste of time, and nothing untoward in any way occurred. We know this because there were several other attendees at the meeting. One of them was Anatoli Samochornov, a Russian-born U.S. citizen who works as a project manager for the Meridian International Center deployed to the U.S. Mission at the United Nations. Samochornov also worked part-time as an interpreter, and it was in that capacity that he joined the conference at Trump Tower.

In early March 2020, a bunch of FBI 302s—the summaries of interviews provided by FBI agents—were declassified. Among them was a write-up of an FBI interview with Samochornov, arguably the one person in Trump Jr.'s office who had nothing to lose or gain by the subjects discussed in the meeting. His agenda was to translate the proceeding, file an invoice, and get paid. Yes, he had worked with Natalia Veselnitskaya on a civil litigation case involving the frozen assets of a company called Prevezon Holdings, translating depositions for her since October 2015. Other than that business relationship, he had no horse in this race.

According to the FBI summary, agents interviewed Samochornov at his home in Rockland County, NY, and he was apparently very forthcoming, even telling them that he had just poured himself a glass of scotch.

Samochornov recounted his career as a translator to the FBI agents, he talked about his previous work with Veselnitskaya, and he even mentioned that he dined at Nello—the super-pricey East Side eatery that one restaurant critic described as "Oligarchic chic"[5]—with Veselnitskaya just hours before the Trump Tower meeting, and said the approaching meeting was never discussed.

Here, however, is the key part of the 302:

> Samochornov could not speak for other occasions but said there was no discussion about the 2016 United States presidential election or collusion between the Russian government and the Trump campaign at the meeting, there was no smoking gun according to Samochornov. There was not a discussion about "dirt" on Hillary Clinton. Samochornov did not think Hillary Clinton was mentioned by name at the meeting. Samochornov had not heard Veselnitskaya say anything about having "dirt" on Hillary Clinton. Samochornov did not offer any materials during the meeting and no papers were exchanged. Additionally, there was no follow-up to the meeting that Samochornov knows about.[6]

This section is also important:

> Samochornov was not particularly fond of Donald Trump Junior, but stated Donald Trump Jr.'s account of the meeting with Veselnitskaya, as portrayed in recent media reports, was accurate. Samochornov concurred with Donald Trump Junior's account of the meeting. He added, "they were telling the truth."[7]

The 302 reveals plenty of other material for anyone fascinated by the nuts and bolts of this insane episode, including that while Samochornov didn't think Veselnitskaya was employed by the Russian government, he did think she might have connections via the prosecutor general of Russia and the former transportation minister of Moscow, Peter Katsyv—who, by the way, is also the owner of Prevezon Holdings, which was ordered to pay a $5.9 million settlement for tax fraud issues.[8] But the 302 passages I just excerpted basically show what a witch hunt and charade this "scandal" was.

Just days after the story broke, the FBI determined that the one guy in the entire affair—a guy who was on record saying he didn't particularly like Trump Jr. and wasn't even working for the campaign—said Hillary Clinton was never discussed and no dirt on Clinton was exchanged. In other words, there was not one iota of collusion at this meeting.

None. Zero. Nada. Nothing.

Let's spell it out: N-O C-O-L-L-U-S-I-O-N.

Mueller must have known this. Why did he continue investigating? Did his hopeless investigators think that somehow a "secret code" was being spoken in Russian and English that only Veselnitskaya and Trump Jr. could understand? Did they suspect "secret documents" were somehow passed—and a roomful of people didn't notice anything? Some, like ex-CIA official John Sipher, have absurdly speculated that this might have been the first approach of a more intricate operation.[9] But there was no follow-up meeting.

So why did this "story" continue to spread like wildfire and why did Mueller refuse to douse conspiracy theorists and scandalmongers?

In order to answer this, I have to back up slightly and return to our pal Glenn Simpson, the omnipresent operator who dined with Veselnitskaya *the night before and the night after the Trump Tower meeting.*

Simpson and Fusion GPS were working with Veselnitskaya on the Prevezon Holdings Limited issues that brought the Russian lawyer to the U.S. Incredibly, the consummate DC swamp rat says his client never mentioned the meeting with the son, son-in-law, and campaign chairman of the presumptive Republican candidate for president of the United States. Remember: the convention was just ten days away. Suffice it to say, I don't trust Simpson as far as I can throw him.

Nobody has been more invested in spinning the Trump-Russia collusion story than Glenn Simpson. He is Christopher Steele's paymaster. He is Paul Manafort's stalker. His connections to anti-Trump media hounds like Michael Isikoff are well documented. And, as I pointed out in the previous chapter, he has made *millions of dollars* for Fusion GPS, trying to float Russia-collusion stories.

And so with that in mind, let's look at the sourcing and timing behind how the *New York Times* broke this non-story. The so-called paper of record has been the leader in trumpeting innuendo-filled tales about the Trump campaign that go absolutely nowhere and achieve nothing beyond publicizing the many pointless investigations by the FBI and Robert Mueller. The Trump Tower meeting story is a prime example.

The entire story is based on "confidential government records described to the *New York Times.*" Who described those records and related interviews? "People familiar with them."[10]

Yes, this broad wording makes it possible that the *Times*'s sources could have been meeting attendees who were interviewed by investigators, or maybe their lawyers. The "confidential government records" could have been copies of emails and texts, for all we know. In fact, given that the *Times* obtained copies of Goldstone and Trump Jr.'s emails within days of the first article, this seems pretty likely.

But the *Times* has displayed a knack for getting inside information that is only available through law enforcement channels. And unless it is using "government records" to create misdirection, the details once again point to a source with ties to the special counsel's office or the FBI. Or both.

Why would operatives from these offices want to leak this story? Especially a story that leads nowhere. In terms of a "gotcha" outcome, the leaks don't make sense because the investigators knew nothing was discussed. Usually, the only thing that matters to law enforcement is the end result. Nobody brags about an indictment when it fails to end in a conviction. There are no after-trial toasts that say, "Well, we almost got 'em!" Seen in that light, this entire episode has been a public relations embarrassment.

So, what was the point of the meeting and what was the point, a year later, of leaking the meeting?

Let's start with the first question: I've said this on my podcast and I'll say it again: Veselnitskaya didn't have *anything* on Hillary Clinton. She wasn't there to give the Trump team fake information on Hillary. Or real information, for that matter. (And if she had given the Trump team fake information that was later discovered to be fake, the Trump team would have figured out this was a scam.) Veselnitskaya's only purpose was to just show up. That's it. She didn't even have to mention Hillary's name. The presence of a well-connected Russian lawyer in Trump Tower was the only thing required to plant a story in the media and reap a scandal of national proportions.

The meeting was the evidence.

It provided the optics, the soundbites, the cast, and the characters to create the appearance of a scandal.

All that was needed was a picture of Veselnitskaya entering Trump Tower or an email about the meeting, and, like magic—abracadabra!— you've got all the necessary elements for a screaming headline about a collusion scandal:

"**Bombshell Revelation: Kremlin-Linked Lawyer Met with Trump, Jr.!**"

(*Pssst: Right before the Republican Convention.*)

And that is exactly what happened.

Thanks to the FBI 302 on translator Samochornov, we know the meeting should have been the beginning, the middle, and the end of the entire Trump Tower story. It wasn't worth a single article, never mind the thousands it generated. Instead, it stands as one of the biggest non-stories ever broken by the *New York Times*. A joke. Twenty minutes of wasted time that devolved into an attempt to destabilize the Trump administration.

As for who engineered this meeting and realized the damaging optics it would cause? Veselnitskaya had contacts with two organizations that were invested in actively destabilizing Trump: Russian oligarchs on one side, and Fusion GPS, which hated oligarchs, on the other. Either party is not beyond instigating the meeting and then watching the damage unfold. Veselnitskaya, it turns out, was hardly a model citizen; in 2019, she was indicted in New York for obstructing a federal investigation into the Prevezon Holdings money laundering scheme that brought her to the U.S. in the first place.[11] Veselnitskaya also admitted in an NBC interview that she had worked with a military unit with ties to Soviet intelligence and was a source for the Russian prosecutor general, Yuri Y. Chaika.[12] She was charged with fabricating evidence and collaborating with Chaika's office to write an official letter that benefited Prevezon. If she's not beneath manufacturing evidence, taking part in a meeting based on a bogus premise would easily be in her wheelhouse.

Meanwhile, it is worth noting that everything Simpson touched has leaked in some way. His employment deal with the DNC; his hiring of Nellie Ohr, wife of Associate Deputy Attorney General Bruce Ohr, to conduct research on oligarchs; the dossier he hired Christopher Steele to compile. All of this made its way into the media in a matter of months. Waiting an entire year to blow the whistle hasn't been Simpson's style. But who knows when it comes to the swamp king?

One more thing about Simpson's "employer" Veselnitskaya and her interpreter Samochornov. Buried on page 123 of the Mueller Report is a reference to a second FBI 302 with Samochornov dated July 13, 2017—a day after the first FBI interview summary. Per the Mueller Report, Veselnitskaya's backers offered to pay big bucks to Samochornov if he corroborated Veselnitskaya's version of events. Here, read it for yourself:

> Specifically, the organization that hired Samochornov—an anti-Magnitsky Act group controlled by Veselnitskaya and the owner of Prevezon—offered to pay $90,000 of Samochornov's legal fees. At Veselnitskaya's request, the organization sent Samochornov a transcript of a Veselnitskaya press interview, and Samochornov understood that the organization would pay his legal fees only if he made statements consistent with Veselnitskaya's. Samochornov declined, telling the Office that he did not want to perjure himself.[13]

That is what you call collusion. It's amazing but not surprising the media didn't leap on this. It shows Glenn Simpson's Russian contract employer working to undermine an FBI investigation. It's like these people are trying to out-slime each other. Like they are playing a game of unethical limbo—how low can you go?

When it comes to who leaked and promoted this non-event, however, the answer gets much clearer. The only people who benefited were the ones invested in creating Spygate and building a collusion case against Donald Trump: Deputy Attorney General Rod Rosenstein, who was overseeing the Russiagate probe, and his own personal hero, Robert Mueller. The second reason—the *real* reason this story was leaked—was because Mueller needed it out there. By having the media printing and broadcasting sinister-sounding allegations, they provided the witch hunt with legitimizing cover and media stories to generate public rage and anger. On July 12, the FBI knew there was no collusion after Samochornov told them everything. But the Mueller team suppressed this evidence and instead obtained a search warrant for the communications, records, and documents from all the attendees of the June 9, 2016, meeting at Trump Tower.

Mueller was appointed special counsel on May 17, 2017, "to oversee the previously-confirmed FBI investigation of Russian government efforts to influence the 2016 presidential election and related matters," as the Department of Justice press release put it.[14] So when July 2017 hit, he had already had six weeks to figure out just what "hard" evidence of collusion existed.

And he'd determined it was pretty damn flimsy.

Faced with this realization, Mueller's team went all in. He needed to create the impression that the Trump collusion story—which was literally fiction—was the gravest threat to America since Watergate. So less than two months into his investigation, and to save the reputation of his beloved FBI by proving the campaign was out of control, he told his team to pull out all the stops. Like legal alchemists, they would somehow apply legal pressure to magically turn fantasy into reality. In terms of Russiagate headlines, no month was hotter than July. Here's what went down.

The meeting at Trump Tower was leaked, Donald Trump Jr. was forced to release a few embarrassing emails, and a slew of campaign figures and prominent Russians would now go under the prosecutors' microscope. The best way to shut people up? Make them think they are at risk of an indictment.

On July 26, the FBI staged a pre-dawn raid on Paul Manafort's home in Alexandria. It was a nasty, get-tough raid. Subpoenas to obtain Manafort's records had already been issued. But nothing says "We think you are guilty" like a shock-and-awe raid. And subpoenas just aren't as dramatic as TV images of agents in FBI jackets carrying computers out of a house.

The next day, July 27, disturbing text messages between senior FBI agent Peter Strzok and high-level FBI lawyer Lisa Page were forwarded to FBI Deputy Director Andrew McCabe from DOJ Inspector General Horowitz. These communications revealed the information-laundering operation behind the dossier and forced Mueller to understand that the FBI investigators had nothing on the Trump team either. In Strzok's own words, "There was no there there." And that means that the real case wasn't about Trump-Russia collusion, it was about some bad apples in the law enforcement and intelligence communities running spy operations on Donald Trump and his campaign. McCabe then immediately pulled Strzok off Mueller's crack investigative team.

But Mueller and his team doubled down even more. That same day, FBI agents were at it again, greeting George Papadopoulos at the airport. You remember Papadopoulos, right? He was the youngest advisor on the Trump team who, according to the FBI timeline, kicked off Operation Crossfire Hurricane by allegedly telling Alexander Downer, the former Australian High Commissioner to the UK, that Russians had some kind of damaging material about Hillary Clinton. Papadopoulos claimed he has no memory of saying this. And multiple efforts by the FBI to use informants to "catch" Papadopoulos in some kind of incriminating statement, including the use of former CIA asset and FBI source Stefan Halper and a mysterious honeypot spy, had failed. Not only failed, but when transcripts emerged in April 2020 of Papadopoulos's late 2016 conversations with an FBI spy targeting him, the transcripts were exculpatory, as Papadopoulos repeatedly denied any collusion efforts with Russians. But the airport meeting was the bureau's last attempt to really nail him. According to Papadopoulos's book, *Deep State Target*, the investigators rifled through his luggage repeatedly and seemed very frustrated by the results of their search.[15] Were they looking for the $10,000 in cash, which Papadopoulos had left in Greece? Did they think he would bring that money into the country without declaring it, making him vulnerable to serious charges and huge fines? It sure seemed like it to Papadopoulos, who was placed under arrest.

The next day, Mueller's vaunted prosecutors were late filing charges against their new target. When they showed up, they hit him with two charges of lying to an FBI agent and obstruction of justice that could have been ready months earlier. Mueller and company were hoping to file much heavier charges to really put pressure on Papadopoulos to flip on members of Trump's campaign and save himself. But when he showed up at the airport cashless, that avenue was closed off, leading to a quickie arrest on other charges.[16]

This same day, news broke that top FBI lawyer James Baker was under investigation for leaking Russiagate information to the media.[17] We know that this was also the month that Mueller's team stretched its net, contacting General Michael Flynn and his family for the first time, and putting former Trump personal attorney Michael Cohen in its sights.

But of all this summer fun, nothing came close to creating the damning optics of meeting with a real live Russian with ties to Russian intelligence at Trump Tower. Yes, the Manafort raid was impressive. It gave the impression of Mueller zeroing in on the Trump campaign chairman. But that was nothing compared to Trump's own son and son-in-law taking a meeting in which they hoped to get intel on Hillary Clinton. That was the golden ticket to prove collusion. And even though Mueller knew it didn't happen—because the translator in the room, who had no horse in this race, said it didn't—the special counsel prosecutors played it to the hilt, knowing it would make life that much harder for the president and hoping it would create pressure that would lead to a breakthrough that would let them prove a case that was unprovable.

Of course, they couldn't do it. Not even after spending $32 million of taxpayers' money on the investigation and its epic encyclopedia of empty allegations, the Mueller Report. But that's because you can't buy proof that never existed.

The biggest outrage of all this goes back to Mueller failing to prosecute or even build a case against the real collusion that had taken place during the campaign—the hiring of Fusion GPS by Clinton and the DNC and the use of Christopher Steele to fabricate proof of collusion. Steele claimed that he relied on Russian sources and sources with close ties to Russia to bolster his dossier, which alleged the Trump campaign was working with Russia to hurt Clinton. But if you reverse engineer all that, it's clear the Clinton campaign was using this research to hurt Trump.

I noted grave concerns about Steele's sources in *Exonerated*, including the fact that notes from his October 2016 meeting with Deputy Assistant Secretary of State Kathleen Kavalec indicated that the dossier author mentioned his sources included Russian spymaster Vyacheslav Trubnikov and former Putin pal Vladislav Surkov, two men who would have wanted to spin Steele like a top.

The inspector general's 2019 report is equally damning of Steele's shoddy work. It quotes Steele's main source as saying Steele "misstated or exaggerated" information provided to him, and that he did not provide one sensational claim attributed to him—that Carter Page had been offered a brokerage fee in the sale of part of the Russian oil giant Rosneft.

The IG report also dismisses Steele's bogus allegation claiming Trump fixer Michael Cohen flew to Prague to meet with Russian hackers.[18]

All these lies and rumors didn't hurt Clinton. They hurt Trump. But Mueller to this day has given the Steele dossier a pass. It is barely mentioned in the Mueller Report—a document that rambled on and on about the Trump Tower meeting for thirteen pages before concluding that—cue the drum roll—nothing happened.

CHAPTER 3

Brennan Unmasked

CIA's primary mission is to collect, analyze, evaluate, and disseminate foreign intelligence to assist the President and senior US government policymakers in making decisions relating to national security. This is a very complex process and involves a variety of steps.

First, we have to identify a problem or an issue of national security concern to the US government. In some cases, CIA is directed to study an intelligence issue—such as what activities terrorist organizations are planning, or how countries that have biological or chemical weapons plan to use these weapons—then we look for a way to collect information about the problem.

There are several ways to collect information. Translating foreign newspaper and magazine articles and radio and television broadcasts provides open-source intelligence. Imagery satellites take pictures from space, and imagery analysts write reports about what they see—for example, how many airplanes are at a foreign military base. Signals analysts work to decrypt coded messages sent by other countries. Operations officers recruit foreigners to give information about their countries.

After the information is collected, intelligence analysts pull together the relevant information from all available sources and assess what is happening, why it is happening, what might occur next, and what it means for US interests. The result of this analytic effort is timely and objective assessments, free of any political bias, provided to senior US policymakers in the form of finished intelligence products that include written reports and oral briefings.

...It is also important to know that the CIA is not a law enforcement organization. That is the job of the FBI; however, the CIA and the FBI cooperate on a number of issues, such as counterintelligence and counterterrorism.

—"What We Do," About the CIA[1]

John Brennan, the CIA director in the Obama administration, has a lot of explaining to do.

The former director has never met an anti-Trump tweet he didn't like and infamously launched many of his own, including one that accused Trump of being "wholly in the pocket of Putin" and charged that the president's Helsinki press conference "rises to & exceeds the threshold of 'high crimes & misdemeanors.'"[2]

But Brennan's behavior and political biases become more problematic in light of questions surrounding his organization's role in collecting and analyzing intelligence that promoted the Russiagate collusion storyline that he so ardently sold to the media.

In May 2019, Attorney General William Barr assigned John H. Durham, the United States attorney in the District of Connecticut, to examine the origins of the Russia investigation. Durham was said to be interested in how the intelligence community determined that Russia actively sought to work with and help Mr. Trump defeat Hillary Clinton in the 2016 election. Or, to borrow from the CIA's own language, how the agency assessed what was happening, why it was happening, what might have occurred next, and what it meant for U.S. interests.

In essence, Durham, like the Department of Justice Inspector General Michael Horowitz, was tasked with delving into many of the conflicts, protocol violations, and abuses of power that I have documented on my podcast and previous books.

When news of Durham's appointment broke, Brennan called it "silly." "Is there a criminal investigation now on analytic judgments and the activities of CIA in terms of trying to protect our national security?" he asked. "I'm certainly willing to talk to Mr. Durham or anybody else who has any questions about what we did during this period of 2016."[3]

Just how much he will talk or how honestly remains to be seen. As the former head of America's top cloak-and-dagger agency, he will likely hide behind claims of national security.

But there is plenty of evidence to suggest that despite the self-professed intention that "the CIA and the FBI cooperate on a number of issues," as the agency's web page states, Brennan's agency failed to share information and may, in fact, have been laundering suspect foreign intelligence to drum up support for a bogus collusion narrative.

INTELLIGENCE DESIGN?

According to various reports, the January 6, 2017, Intelligence Community Assessment (ICA) overseen by Brennan and National Intelligence Director James Clapper is high on Durham's inquiry list. This document aggregated a good deal of publicly available information about Russian strategic interests. It documented Russian news outlets and government figures being extremely critical of Hillary Clinton. More salient, and not as widely known, were assessments asserting, "The Kremlin's campaign aimed at the US election featured disclosures of data obtained through Russian cyber operations; intrusions into US state and local electoral boards; and overt propaganda. Russian intelligence collection both informed and enabled the influence campaign."

The key takeaway of the assessment was the conclusion "with high confidence that Russian President Vladimir Putin ordered an influence campaign in 2016 aimed at the US presidential election, the consistent goals of which were to undermine public faith in the US democratic process, denigrate Secretary Clinton, and harm her electability and potential presidency."[4]

For the record, there was one dissenting voice. Admiral Mike Rogers, the head of the National Security Agency, had only "moderate confidence" that Putin actively tried to help Trump win and Clinton lose. "It didn't have the same level of sourcing and the same level of multiple sources," Rogers told the Senate in 2017. "I'd call it an honest difference of opinion between three different organizations."[5]

But the assessment also contained one telling paragraph that the intelligence officials seemed to have forgotten about.

> **By their nature, Russian influence campaigns are multifaceted and designed to be deniable because they use a mix of agents of influence, cutouts, front organizations, *and false-flag operations*.**

I italicized that last phrase for emphasis. False-flag operations are orchestrated misdirection campaigns usually rooted in elaborate misrepresentations. For example, if one country, let's call it Evilstan, wanted to start a war between Democroland and Peacenovia, they might hire a ship, hoist up a Democroland flag (a false flag, get it?), and then bomb a Peacenovia vessel. Evilstan is the bad guy here, but its sinister operation was designed to make Democroland look like the bad guy.

Here's the thing: there's not much difference between false-flag operations and disinformation campaigns. They both involve strategic lying to influence or achieve a desired outcome. And there was unquestionably misinformation floating around in the CIA and FBI. And it was very likely the result of an active disinformation campaign. So, it is painfully ironic that the Intelligence Community Assessment noted this possibility and then completely ignored it when demonstrably false information—the Steele dossier—was inserted into the investigation. As I have pointed out for years, the Steele dossier wasn't worth the paper it was printed on. IG Horowitz has been damning about how the unverified Steele dossier was used to justify FISA warrants against Trump campaign team member Carter Page.

In April 2020, newly declassified footnotes from the Horowitz report revealed the FBI was warned that allegations in Steele's report could have been planted by Russia. The details are both stunning and damning, confirming that much of the dossier was utterly suspect.

Footnote 350 in the IG report, which delves into the FBI's knowledge about the Russian contacts that fueled Steele's reports, notes that the former MI6 operative's files were completely suspect:

> In addition to the information in Steele's Delta file documenting Steele's frequent contacts with representatives for multiple Russian oligarchs, we identified reporting the Crossfire Hurricane team received from [redacted] indicating the potential for Russian disinformation influencing Steele's election reporting. A January 12, 2017, report relayed information from [redacted] outlining an inaccuracy in a limited subset of Steele's reporting about the activities of Michael Cohen. The [redacted] stated that it did not have high confidence in this subset of Steele's reporting and assessed that the referenced subset was part of a Russian disinformation campaign to denigrate U.S. foreign relations....[6]

The suggestion that Steele had been duped by Russian intelligence services (RIS) surfaced again just as Trump assumed office. "In late January 2017, a member of the Crossfire Hurricane team received information [redacted] that RIS may have targeted Orbis [Steele's firm]," reveals footnote 342, which goes on to deliver more tip-off news: "An early June 2017 USIC report indicated that two persons affiliated with RIS were aware of Steele's election investigation in early July 2016. The Supervisory Intel Analyst told us he was aware of these reports, but that he had no information as of June 2017 that Steele's election reporting source network had been penetrated or compromised."[7]

This last statement reveals what a clown show this was, with the left hand remaining utterly clueless about what the right was doing. This supervisory intel analyst's claim is contradicted by footnote 211, which states that intelligence suggesting Steele's operation was compromised arrived in the early days of the Mueller investigation *in June 2017*. "Sensitive source reporting from June 2017 indicated that a Person affiliated to Russian Oligarch 1 was possibly aware of Steele's election investigation as of early July 2016."[8]

Maybe the supervisor missed that report. Maybe he forgot about it. But don't tell me there was nothing to indicate Steele's operation may have been targeted by the Russians. The absurd and outrageous claims in the dossier itself should have been a tip-off. So should the murky, nonspecific sourcing. And the FBI and other intelligence divisions at the very least suspected the dossier was bogus because they were warned the Russians knew about Steele. They just decided to ignore it.

Why let facts or suspicions get in the way of a good conspiracy, right?

SCANDAL LAUNDERING

Clapper, Brennan, Comey, and Rogers decided to attach a summary of the unverified dossier to the end of the ICA that was given to President Obama on January 5. The fact that the FBI and CIA (the IG report sourced a dossier tip-off to the USIC, which is likely the CIA) had been told the dossier probably contained compromised intel makes this decision even sleazier than anyone imagined. Think about it: Rumors that were created by Russian intelligence were spoon-fed to Steele, who was hired by political operatives working for Hillary Clinton. Steele then fed these fictions to the FBI, attributing the claims to real people who, according to the inspector general's report, subsequently denied knowledge of the information, or insisted they stated it was rumor and innuendo. The FBI knew Steele's report might be disinformation. Everybody knew. But they included it anyway.

Given all that, it's pathetic that Brennan and the FBI's *best-case* explanation of their malfeasance is to suggest that they were unwittingly fooled by Russian Intelligence and wound up placing disinformation on the president's desk.

The reality is that this decision nearly destroyed the Trump presidency. Presenting the dossier to Obama, as I'll explain, gave Steele's pack of lies a deceptive sheen of legitimacy, essentially detonating the entire Spygate fiasco to play out in public and cripple the Trump presidency.

In 2019, after the Steele dossier was exposed as utter garbage and Durham was appointed to probe the genesis of the investigation, backers of Brennan and former FBI head James Comey shifted into overdrive to shield their bosses. One anonymous CIA operative placed the blame firmly on Comey, insisting Brennan and Clapper "opposed James Comey's recommendation that the Steele Dossier be included in the intelligence report." Meanwhile, Fox News reported that sources claimed a late 2016 email chain indicated Comey told FBI staffers that Brennan insisted the dossier be included. The conclusion of this "he said-he said" battle will be interesting. Based on bile-spewing Brennan's Trump attacks, I believe he is the odds-on favorite as the biggest dossier-backer. But there is other supporting evidence including statements from Rand Paul, a Senate Committee on Foreign Relations member, and Trey Gowdy, the former House Judiciary Committee Chairman, that suggest it was Brennan. Then there is reason to believe the CIA had its own back channel evidence that the FBI didn't know about. According to sworn testimony, members of the FBI self-professed anti-Trumpers were shocked to discover this and became convinced their covert counterparts were playing games slandering the presidential candidate.

This is a complicated three-part story. But here are the plot lines.

1. How the CIA learned of supposed "collusion" and how Brennan pushed this story out to members of Congress and the Obama administration.

2. How texts between two FBI lovebirds, lawyer Lisa Page and counter-intel supervisor Peter Strzok, indicate that the CIA was pushing a collusion narrative that wasn't true.

3. How testimony by Lisa Page indicates Brennan's team was conducting its own operations to push a storyline.

BRENNAN'S FOLLIES

In 2015, more than a year before John Brennan left the CIA to become the most unhinged Never-Trump member of the Obama administration, his agency was receiving intelligence about "figures connected to Trump and known or suspected Russian agents," the *Guardian* reported.[9]

Months later, an intelligence report about an alleged recording that mentioned Moscow payments "going into the US presidential campaign" was funneled to Brennan in April 2016, according to the BBC,[10] by which time Trump was the firm favorite to nab the Republican nomination. These reports have never been corrected or retracted, and Brennan appeared to confirm them in testimony to Congress.

"I encountered and am aware of information and intelligence that revealed contacts and interactions between Russian officials and U.S. persons involved in the Trump campaign that I was concerned about because of known Russian efforts to suborn such individuals," he told the House Intelligence Committee on May 23, 2017.

"It raised questions in my mind about whether Russia was able to gain the cooperation of those individuals," he said, adding, "I don't know whether such collusion existed."[11]

We still don't know who, exactly, provided this intelligence, what the specific details were, or when it was delivered. Brennan has never shared this information. But some candidates have emerged. Intelligence agents don't exist in a vacuum. They are parts of big organizations with multiple divisions and subdivisions. Many operators in the profession move into the private sector, their value enhanced because their connections to the government agencies remain in place. It is the way of the Swamp. So, bear that in mind as you read the following facts:

- In June 2016, the FBI claimed it was informed of Australian High Commissioner Alexander Downer's report that Trump advisor George Papadopoulos had told him during a London May meeting that the Russians had material that would be used to sink Hillary Clinton. (A text exchange between the FBI investigator Strzok and FBI lawyer Lisa Page on May 11, a day after the Downer-Papadopoulos meeting, about "affidavits" being prepped and calls with "State" lead me to believe that the FBI likely knew about the Downer meeting much earlier.) That, according to the *official* timeline of the FBI, caused the launch of Operation Crossfire Hurricane, the investigation into Russian influencing of the 2016 election.

- In June 2016, former MI6 Russia specialist Christopher Steele was formally engaged by Glenn Simpson of Fusion GPS to conduct opposition research. The first entry to his dossier was dated June 20, 2016. One year earlier, Simpson was approached by a former CIA analyst named Nellie Ohr, who spoke Russian. He hired her.[12]

- Steele met and briefed his Department of Justice pal Bruce Ohr and his wife, Nellie Ohr, on the dossier over breakfast at the Mayflower Hotel on July 30, 2016.[13]

- In early July, Steele was also sharing his work with FBI contact Michael Gaeta in Rome, Italy.[14]

- On December 3, 2016, Steele and Christopher Burrows, a former British agent who started Orbis with Steele, met with Sir Richard Dearlove, their former boss at MI6, at London's posh Garrick Club. There, they presented Dearlove with a copy of the dossier. After reading the document, according to Glenn Simpson, Dearlove pronounced it credible and indicated "that he was already aware that the British government had suspicions about links between Russia and members of the Trump campaign."[15]

- Dearlove is a friend and colleague of U.S. intelligence asset Stefan Halper, who has also been a source for the FBI. Dearlove and Halper both have multiple connections to Hakluyt, a strategic intelligence firm founded by ex-MI6 agents. Alexander Downer served on the Advisory Board of Hakluyt until 2014.

- Halper was used by the FBI to befriend, and spy on, both Carter Page and George Papadopoulos. (Halper also figures heavily in my chapter about the takedown of Mike Flynn, so keep him in the back of your mind—nearly everyone in this scandal-palooza is connected.)

- All these facts point to one thing: months and months before the National Intelligence Assessment was presented, there were multiple vectors for the CIA to pick up on Steele's bogus reports. We know Brennan was getting intel from his unnamed foreign sources, but even if he wasn't, this disinformation was circulating widely. Steele himself was circulating it. Dearlove, who was no longer officially tied to MI6, had heard about Steele's collusion plotlines before Steele showed them to him! Nellie Ohr, who shared an employer with Steele—not to mention a breakfast briefing from him—had multiple connections to The Company. Given the explosive nature of the rumors Steele was peddling and the fact that Australian, British, and other intelligence agencies frequently share information with U.S. intelligence under the "Five Eyes" agreement, it would be a miracle if news of the dossier hadn't made it to Brennan.

By August 2016, nearly two months after the *Washington Post* first reported that the Democratic National Committee had been attacked by Russian hackers,[16] the Never-Trump CIA director appears to have reached his paranoid peak, reportedly calling eight senior members from Capitol Hill. On August 25, he briefed Harry Reid, then the top Democratic Party senator, and "indicated that Russia's hackings appeared aimed at helping Mr. Trump win the November election," according to the *New York Times*, which also reported, "Brennan also indicated that unnamed advisers to Mr. Trump might be working with the Russians to interfere in the election."[17]

The Reid briefing compelled the Nevada senator to write and release a letter to FBI head James Comey on August 27, alerting him that "the evidence of a direct connection between the Russian government and Donald Trump's presidential campaign continues to mount." He also urged the FBI director to "use every resource available" to investigate possible election interference.[18]

Brennan understood the cause-and-effect mechanisms that drive news cycles. Briefings pumped up the pressure on Trump precisely because citizens of the Swamp would write letters and release statements that cast the shadow of collusion on the campaign. California's leading Capitol Hill windbags, Senator Dianne Feinstein and Representative Adam Schiff, predictably added to the Brennan-boosted assault in a joint statement: "Based on briefings we have received, we have concluded that the Russian intelligence agencies are making a serious and concerted effort to influence the U.S. election."[19]

The crescendo of Brennan's bogus Trump trashing occurred on January 5, 2017, when Clapper, Comey, Brennan, and then-NSA Director Michael Rogers briefed the ICA report to President Obama. By this time, the CIA and FBI had shared the dossier, which resulted in a good deal of internal debate about whether to include the Steele dossier in the ICA. Comey loyalist Andrew McCabe made a big push to include it, according to the inspector general's report, while a CIA analyst said that "they believed that the Steele election reporting was not completely vetted and did not merit inclusion in the body of the report."[20]

Somewhere along the way, the idea of an appendix surfaced. Comey remembered the decision this way:

> I think I was just told, in, I think, in a meeting with Clapper and Brennan and [then NSA Director] Rogers, that the IC analysts found it credible on its face and gravamen of it, and consistent with our other information, but not in a position where they would integrate it into the IC assessment. But they thought it was important enough and consistent enough that it ought to be part of the package in some way, and so they had come up with this idea to make an [appendix].[21]

Brennan, for his part, appeared on *Meet the Press* on February 4, 2018, and said the dossier "was not a very well-kept secret among press circles for several months before it came out. It was late summer 2016 and there were some individuals from the various US news outlets who asked me about my familiarity with it. I had heard just snippets about it. I did not know what was in there. I did not see it until later in that year, I think it was in December." In the same interview, he also stated that *the Steele dossier did not figure into the ICA.* "I was unaware of the provenance of it as well as what was in it," he told *Meet the Press.* "And it did not play any role whatsoever in the intelligence community's assessment that was done, that was presented to then-President Obama and then-President-elect Trump."[22]

But Comey's quote, as well as further information in the IG report, indicates Brennan was lying. The three intelligence veterans and their ostensible overseer, James Clapper, also decided to present the ICA to President-elect Trump, and designated Comey to present the salacious and outrageous fictional sexcapades described in the dossier to Trump. "Comey stated that the other USIC Directors agreed that Trump had to be briefed on this information, and Clapper decided the briefing should be done by Comey in a small group or alone with the President-elect."[23]

So, the decision to present the dossier was a group effort. But which of the four men in this group had a track record on sharing information and then watching it wind up in the media? Rogers was a choir boy compared to the others. Comey, of course, started doing this when he found himself in the hot seat and was booted from office. But only Brennan, as far as we know, was truly gifted at intelligence laundering and the fine art of show-and-tell-and-leaking.

After the Steele scandal sheet was presented to Trump, all hell broke loose. It provided an excuse for the media to report on unverified rumors. It provided an excuse for Buzzfeed to publish the entire, fantasy-filled document, conferring a piece of truth-challenged trash with an undeserved aura of spy-versus-spy legitimacy.

The ICA didn't just turn up the dial on a simmering scandal. In many regards, it detonated the entire Spygate fiasco. It resulted in turning Steele's sky-is-falling collusion fantasy into a primetime scandal that nearly crippled the Trump presidency.

THE FBI CONNECTION

When Brennan claimed on *Meet the Press* that he first saw the dossier in December and that it didn't factor into the ICA, he wasn't just lying; he was basically throwing the FBI under the bus. The man who had raised the alarm for months and whose staff traveled in the same spy world circles as Christopher Steele was essentially saying that determining the veracity of the election interference and collusion rumors he had shared with Harry Reid, Adam Schiff, and others on Capitol Hill was the responsibility of the FBI.

Excuse me? It is not the job of the outgoing head of the CIA to share and spread unverified rumors to damage the president-elect of the United States. Brennan, in this instance, forgot the disinformation warning that is part and parcel of CIA policy.

What a disgrace. The so-called spymaster was duped.

Or was he?

Brennan's whisper campaign may have served another purpose. He was spreading unverified rumors. So was Steele. If Brennan had heard Steele's information, if Steele's fabrications made it into intel communiques and Brennan was repeating them, or, worse, if Brennan actually was in touch with people who were in touch with Steele, well, then the two men were effectively working to verify each other's rumors.

When Jim Comey or Harry Reid learned about Steele's lie-filled dossier information, they would have good reason to think his flimsy fables were true—because *they'd heard the same thing from the head of the CIA.*

Just because two sources tell the same lie doesn't make the lie true. But when two supposedly professional intelligence and law enforcement experts are talking, the incredible may start to sound credible. They are corroborating each other's lies and feeding them through various channels to launder allegations.

Steele and Brennan made the FBI's job harder. Seen in a certain light, you can even appreciate *initially* why Jim Comey and Rod Rosenstein and Robert Mueller would think there might somehow, some way, be some truth to the whole collusion myth.

Disinformation can be very compelling.

It's fitting, then, that two of the key Russiagate figures in all this, FBI lawyer Lisa Page and Peter Strzok, the FBI supervisor who led both the bureau probe into Hillary Clinton's inexcusable use of a private email server and the Crossfire Hurricane investigation, were the ones who ended up shining a light on what Brennan was up to. To be clear, neither Page nor Strzok, who were having an extramarital affair, is a hero in this story. Strzok, who had been part of Robert Mueller's supposed dream team of law enforcement experts, was bounced from that appointment after IG Horowitz examined an avalanche of the couple's texts, which included negative exchanges about Trump. Page resigned in May 2018; Strzok was fired in August of the same year. But their exchanges—over twenty thousand texts—provide fascinating insights into their thinking about the entire Russiagate debacle.

Strzok, in particular, actually provided some of the strongest exculpatory evidence, with his text summing up the entire investigation. It came on May 19, 2017, two days after Robert Mueller was appointed special counsel, and Strzok expressed his ambivalence about joining Mueller's team. "You and I both know the odds are nothing. If I thought it was likely, I'd be there no question. I hesitate in part because of my gut sense and concern is there's no big there there." Boom! It is hard to imagine a more telling statement from a law enforcement figure. I can't emphasize this enough: the man who spent months tracking down collusion leads, the man who probably knew more about the sources and rumors of the entire washout investigation, said he believed there was *"no big there there."*

In other words: No crime. No conspiracy. No collusion.

While that bombshell text makes clear that Strzok thought the Mueller investigation would be a clear and present debacle, another text, written months earlier on October 13, 2016, to Page, indicates he thought other intelligence operatives were playing games. Here's the text:

> We got the reporting on Sept. 19. Looks like [Redacted] got it early August. Looking at [Redacted] lync [an internal messaging service] replies to me it's not clear if he knows if/when he told them. But [Redacted] and [Redacted] talked with [Redacted] they're both good and will remember. It's not about rubbing their nose in it. I don't care if they don't know. I just want to know who's playing games/scared covering.[24]

Let me offer up a partial translation of what I think Strzok was saying and provide some context: *We got the full dossier on Sept. 19. It looks like someone in the intelligence community got the information in early August* [which is when Brennan started whispering to Congress]. *It's not clear if a source knows exactly if or when Steele told the CIA. But two other FBI agents* [possibly Steele's FBI contact in Italy] *will be able to shed light on that.* Strzok ends up by saying he knows everyone will deny previous knowledge and there is no way to prove that the CIA had this intelligence (probably because all the agency intel is classified).

If anyone has any doubts about this translation, read the inspector general's report, which notes that "the Crossfire Hurricane team received the first six election reports on September 19, 2016—more than two months after Steele first gave his handling agent two of the six reports."[25]

So it is crystal clear from Strzok's text that he believes someone else—Brennan?—got the reports in August.

The IG report also says, "Steele directly provided more than a dozen of his reports to the FBI between July and October 2016, and several others to the FBI through [Bruce] Ohr and other third parties."[26] Who were the other third parties? Did any of them have ties to the CIA?

Why was Strzok discussing all this on October 13, 2016? That is a trickier question. But earlier October is the exact time the FBI was preparing its documents for a FISA warrant application for Carter Page, an application that was vital to Crossfire Hurricane because it would allow the bureau to spy on an extended network of people who had been in contact with Page.[27] That FISA application cited the Steele dossier—ignoring the fact that it was an unverified work of total fiction—as compelling evidence to issue the warrant. If I had to guess, it seems like the shady Steele dossier would be front and center in everyone's mind. Especially Peter Strzok, who at some point had doubts about the entire investigation.

The final piece of Brennan-bashing evidence comes from Strzok's paramour, Lisa Page, who testified before the House Judiciary Committee on July 16, 2018. In an exchange with Page, former Rep. Mark Meadows referenced the meeting between Brennan and Harry Reid and said his committee had documents that suggested "in that briefing the dossier was mentioned to Harry Reid."[28]

Page confessed her surprise at this revelation, explaining:

"Because with all due honesty, if director Brennan—so we got that information from our source right? The FBI got this information from our source. If the CIA had another source of that information, I'm neither aware of that nor did the CIA provide it to us."[29]

When Meadows mentioned there "were multiple sources," Page continued:

"I know that, I do know that the information ultimately found its way lots of different places, certainly in October of 2016, but if the CIA as early as August, in fact, had those same reports, I'm not aware of—I'm not aware of that and nor do I believe they provided them to us, and that would be unusual."

Translation: Page is saying if Brennan mentioned the dossier to Reid in August, that would mean Brennan had access to the dossier, which would have been a surprise to Page, because the CIA, if they obtained the dossier, never passed it on to the FBI.

This exchange, in tandem with Strzok's text, is the most damning proof that Brennan was a super-spreader when it came to propagating the collusion storyline that was clearly rooted in a disinformation campaign. Instead of delivering "timely and objective assessments, free of any political bias"—one of the CIA's goals, according to the document that opened this chapter—Brennan delivered rushed, inaccurate, and completely slanted reports of collusion.

It will be very interesting to learn what information Meadows and the House committee had about the Reid meeting. And it will be fascinating to learn what Durham uncovers. In the meantime, published reports say one person with ties to the CIA has hired a lawyer to deal with the Durham probe.

I wonder who that might be?

CHAPTER 4

The National Insecurity Council

On July 26, 2016, President Obama signed something called "Presidential Policy Directive 41—United States Cyber Incident Coordination." The document was an executive order that set forth the "principles governing the Federal Government's response to any cyber incident, whether involving government or private sector entities."[1]

The timing of this directive was curious. The American government and U.S. corporations had been under assault online from hostile attacks launched by foreign entities for decades. American databases, technology assets, and monetary funds have been targeted prey for more than two decades. Cyberwar is a genuine and constant threat. China's army has an entire division devoted to assault operations against the U.S. Iran, North Korea, and other anti-democratic nations launch attacks every day on American assets. They attack citizens, too—email access attacks can be used to execute identity theft, blackmail, and a host of other crimes. In April 2015, the U.S. Office of Personnel Management discovered it had been hacked by Chinese operatives who got away with personal background check data on *more than twenty million Americans*.[2] I remember this vividly because I was on their victim list. My information from when I served as a Secret Service agent had been stolen. Just five months earlier, in November 2014, North Korean hackers launched an utterly crippling attack on Sony Entertainment Pictures, wiping out data, releasing films online, and distributing email and confidential personnel information.

Why didn't President Obama issue his directive in 2015, in the wake of such egregious attacks? Was it incompetence? Cluelessness? Other priorities? Only he can answer that.

It seems clear, however, why he finally got around to issuing this directive when he did. The end of July 2016 was six weeks after the *Washington Post* broke the news of the allegations that the Democratic National Committee had been digitally looted by Russian hackers—an operation, it is alleged, that had been siphoning the email and plans of the DNC for months. The attackers also deployed a basic phishing scheme to steal the private emails of Democrat insider and Hillary lieutenant John Podesta, which were accessed in March 2016.[3]

More to the tipping point, Obama's overdue directive was issued exactly four days *after* Wikileaks published 44,053 emails and 17,761 attachments from numerous Democrat officials.

So, let's look at this sequence of events: In 2014 Sony gets temporarily shut down, and the Treasury eventually sanctions a few North Koreans—*more than three years later.*[4] China steals personal information that can be used to blackmail and influence millions of government workers, *and Obama does nothing.* But when the DNC—the engine that drives Obama's party—is *allegedly* hacked by Russian operatives, the president finally decides it's time to open up a can of whoop-ass?

Make that a *small* can of whoop-ass. Honestly, the directive doesn't go nearly far enough when it comes to protecting our national assets, recovering stolen property, and meting out punishment. Instead, what the directive does, essentially, is say that the government will take large-scale cyberattacks more seriously than it has (okay, thanks!) and codifies the process, going forward, clarifying the federal government's roles and responsibilities. That role includes adhering to five "incidence response" principles. These threat response activities include the law enforcement and national security investigation of a cyber incident, including collecting evidence, linking related incidents, gathering intelligence, identifying opportunities for threat pursuit and disruption, and providing attribution.

To ensure a coordinated response to major cyber incidents, Obama decreed the following:

1. In view of the fact that significant cyber incidents will often involve at least the possibility of a nation-state actor or have some other national security nexus, the Department of Justice, acting through the Federal Bureau of Investigation and the National Cyber Investigative Joint Task Force, shall be the Federal lead agency for threat response activities.

2. The Department of Homeland Security, acting through the National Cybersecurity and Communications Integration Center, shall be the Federal lead agency for asset response activities.

3. The Office of the Director of National Intelligence, through the Cyber Threat Intelligence Integration Center, shall be the Federal lead agency for intelligence support and related activities.[5]

Buried at the end of Clause D in Section III of the directive was an interesting sentence that empowered cyber investigators to work with foreign operatives: "The transnational nature of the Internet and communications infrastructure requires the United States to coordinate with international partners, as appropriate, in managing cyber incidents." This is about as broadly worded a mandate as any investigator could wish for. It's like saying: *FBI: go and work with foreign intelligence services, governments, and you now have a "get out of jail free card" to run down any cyber incident.*

The man designated to ensure the new policy got up and running was Anthony J. Ferrante, the former chief of staff of the FBI's Cyber Division who was Obama's director for Cyber Incident Response at the U.S. National Security Council, a position, according to multiple reports, that made him the FBI's cyber conduit to the White House.

To be clear, that is the same National Security Council where a certain whistleblower worked. The same whistleblower who freaked about Trump's alleged "quid pro quo" conversation with Ukraine President Zelensky and set off the entire impeachment disaster. That whistleblower, as we will document by the end of the book, was an NSC holdover—just like Ferrante—from the Obama administration.

Ferrante's ties to the bureau are interesting because two other events happened on the day Presidential Directive 41 was released. July 26 was the same day that the FBI *claims* foreign intelligence authorities shared Alexander Downer's report alleging that Trump advisor George Papadopoulos told him the Russians had some kind of information that could be used to hurt the Clinton campaign—a claim that Papadopoulos has repeatedly denied. (Again, I am very skeptical about this; suspicious texts between FBI supervisor Peter Strzok and FBI lawyer Lisa Page from the day after Downer met Papadopoulos in early May 2016 appear to contradict the story that the FBI learned of the meeting in July.)

Also on July 26, Christopher Steele drafted "Company Intelligence Report 086," subtitled "A Synopsis of Russian State Sponsored and Other Cyber Offensive (Criminal) Operations." Considering this report was written *after* news of the alleged DNC online infiltration that had been circulating, you could be forgiven if you expected details that filled in the blanks.

Instead, Steele delivered nothing but blanks. Here is his lead "scoop":

> Russia has an extensive programme of state-sponsored offensive cyber operations. External targets include foreign governments and big corporations, especially banks. FSB leads on cyber within Russian apparatus. Limited success in attacking top foreign targets like G7

governments, security services and IFIs [International Financial Institutions] but much more on second tier ones through IT back doors, using corporate and other visitors to Russia.

A high school student armed with Google and a few contemporary spy novels could have come up with this. The FSB, the organization that replaced Putin's beloved KGB, handles internal security and spying operations. Of course they target foreign governments, corporations, and banks. What else would they want to infiltrate? The PTA at my local elementary school? Steele's report talks about attempts to recruit foreign cyber operatives, attempts to plant Trojan horse viruses, and the use of video games to spread malware to gain control of computers and platforms. This intel is astounding because it lacks any specific, or useful, details. Seriously, Glenn Simpson and Steele's Rome-based FBI handler Michael Gaeta should have demanded a refund from the former British spy because his report provides no specifics, which means it *provides no useful information.*

But that didn't matter. It was another alarm bell to add to the chorus of alarms that Simpson and the FBI were teeing up. Look, they had the alleged DNC hack to investigate, Crossfire Hurricane was literally five days from being formally opened, and now Steele was piling on with murky cyber details. It didn't matter if Steele's report was as vague as a three-week-old dream. It was just padding for the BS narrative that needed to be floated to justify investigating Trump and his campaign.

It was a preponderance of unsubstantiated evidence—a.k.a. lies.

Directive #41 not only orders the Department of Justice to take the lead on "threat response activities," it delegates the FBI to spearhead investigations. The directive, in a sense, provides cover for an investigation into Trump-Russia by gluing Steele's cyber misinformation to already established campaign-meddling efforts documented in the alleged DNC online infiltration.

As the NSC's director for Cyber Incident Response and Cybersecurity Policy, and Obama's Directive #41 overseer, Anthony Ferrante had White House access both before and after the 2016 election. So even though he was in the NSC, was he privy to the counterintelligence investigation that was ongoing during the campaign and then remained in place after the Trump administration took over? It may have given him the unique ability to work with the Trump tream while actually helping to investigate it. There has been speculation that Ferrante funneled reports back to the bureau directly to FBI Director James Comey.

The question of whether Ferrante was serving two masters at the NSC remains an open one. A National Security Council official told RealClearInvestigations that Ferrante's position was unprecedented. "Comey created a new FBI reserve position for Ferrante, enabling him to have an ongoing relationship with the agency, retaining his clearances and enabling him to come back in [to bureau headquarters]." The source insisted that "between the election and April 2017, when Ferrante finally left the White House, the Trump NSC division supervisor was not allowed to get rid of Ferrante."[6]

Ferrante left his White House position in April 2017 and took a job as global head of cybersecurity and senior managing director of FTI Consulting, an international business advisory firm with over 3,500 employees. His first reported job, however, was very close to home: he was hired by Buzzfeed to establish the credibility of the Steele dossier, which Buzzfeed infamously published on January 10, 2017.

The site, previously famous for publishing fun and mindless listicles before it embraced publishing Steele's unverified compendium of lies, hired Ferrante because of a hefty libel lawsuit filed by Russian technology executive Aleksej Gubarev. By publishing Steele's creative writing exercise, Buzzfeed had opened itself up to a suit because the dossier included this paragraph, tying Gubarev indirectly to the DNC hack:

> ...a company called XBT/Webzilla and its affiliates had been using
> botnets and porn traffic to transmit viruses, plant bugs, steal data
> and conduct "altering operations" against the Democratic Party

leadership. Entities linked to one Aleksej GUBAROV were involved and he and another hacking expert, both recruited under duress by the FSB, Seva KAPSUGOVICH, were significant players in this operation.[7]

"They can hire Nancy Drew, Encyclopedia Brown, or Sherlock Holmes—you can't find what doesn't exist," Gubarev's lawyer Evan Fray-Witzer explained to a reporter after Buzzfeed brought Ferrante on board. "There is a simple reason why Buzzfeed hasn't found any evidence to support the allegations in the Dossier against Mr. Gubarev: the allegations are false."[8]

The lawyer was 100 percent correct. Ferrante unveiled a forty-page report during the 2018 libel trial that unfolded. Using sophisticated tracking equipment, Ferrante's cyber sleuths had found evidence that Russian agents used networks operated by Mr. Gubarev to start their DNC hack. This was a surprising revelation. Steele, after being wrong time and again, had gotten some information correct. He was batting .001. But Ferrante was unable to directly link Gubarev or senior XBT executives to the hacking. "I have no evidence of them actually sitting behind a keyboard," Ferrante said in a deposition.[9]

While he was working to bolster the reputation of the Steele dossier, Ferrante apparently returned to his old White House stomping grounds. His FBI replacement on the NSC, Jordan Rae Kelly, signed security logs for Ferrante to enter the White House while he was snooping for Buzzfeed.[10] Who does this? I used to work for the Secret Service. It's not like I would get all nostalgic and decide to drop by. Just what Ferrante was doing back at the West Wing while working for Buzzfeed remains an open question. Adding to the mystery is the fact that Kelly, who reportedly had a close working relationship with Mueller, eventually quit the NSC gig and signed on to work at Ferrante's company![11]

Luckily for Buzzfeed, a Florida judge ruled that Gubarev had not proved Buzzfeed had defamed him. Ferrante's monumental effort—he logged thousands of air miles trying to track down proof that Steele's allegations were on the money—fell far short of proving the Steele dossier contained any semblance of truth.

The former FBI cyber sleuth isn't the only one invested in proving Christopher Steele correct. Orbis managing director Arthur Snell came rushing to Steele's defense after a report in an article in London's *Sunday Times* stated the obvious: "There is also a strong possibility that all Steele's material has been fabricated."[12]

"Steele and his company, Orbis Business Intelligence, firmly reject this," Snell wrote in a subsequent rebuttal. "We stand by the integrity and quality of our work."[13]

No surprise there.

Glenn Simpson, another Steele apologist, has revealed that Steele insisted on sharing his reports with the FBI. Eventually, Simpson, who had paid Steele to research and write the dossier, agreed to let Steele contact the bureau. In his book, Simpson offers up an utterly clueless analogy, comparing the act of informing the FBI about unverified rumors of potentially treasonous behavior and sicko pee-pee tapes to seeing a traffic accident and dialing 911.[14] Simpson evidently never considered the damage a false report might do to our nation. And it seems as if he still hasn't reckoned with that idea.

Similarly, Snell tried to justify Steele's efforts to feed his "findings" to U.S. lawmen, claiming it was "solely to assist" the bureau.

"Thereafter Orbis has co-operated extensively with serious U.S. investigations on Russian interference in U.S. elections, with the approval of the U.K. authorities," he added.

This is the most pathetic defense imaginable. All these collusion theorists—card-carrying and honorary members of the Scandal Manufacturers of America—are trying to prove the dossier was correct. Ferrante, Simpson, Snell, Gaeta, and of course the agents working the Operation Crossfire Hurricane. For Orbis to proudly say it cooperated with investigators is absurd. You don't get brownie points for discussing bogus "evidence" with the FBI. And knowingly providing false information to an investigation is a crime. Providing that "information" in order to weaponize a probe meant to discredit a presidential candidate isn't just a crime, it's anti-American. At this point, the dossier is now universally acknowledged as garbage. If any of it held up, it would have been splashed all over the Mueller Report. Instead, it was conspicuously missing in action. The only remaining questions are:

- Was Christopher Steele unwittingly spun like a top by sources or did he suspect any of it was garbage and just shoveled the BS forward anyway?
- And in a related matter, did the FBI know Steele's reports were completely bogus?
- I believe the answer to both questions is yes. Steele knew some of the claims in his report were likely BS lies, and he just decided to shovel it all forward. As for the second question, there is no doubt his sources were spewing lies and, possibly, slivers of Russian disinformation, and that the FBI knew this.

As I rushed to finish this book, several footnotes from IG Horowitz's damning report on FBI behavior were declassified, and the new information shed light on what the FBI really knew about the claims made in Steele's report. Declassified footnote number 350 is particularly devastating and clearly states that, at a minimum, the FBI was aware that Steele's dossier could contain Russian disinformation. Here is the critical language in the footnote: the IG "identified reporting the Crossfire Hurricane team received from REDACTED indicating the potential for Russian disinformation influencing Steele's election reporting."[15] There it is, in black and white. There are only two options here: either the FBI was relying on a document full of outright lies to spy on the Trump team, or the Russians were using Steele, a foreigner, to help Hillary spy on Trump through the FBI. There's no option C.

The footnotes "make clear the FBI possessed information at multiple levels that undercut the evidence it was using to sustain a collusion investigation," a source told reporter John Solomon, just before they were released. It reignited the question of "whether the FBI intentionally ignored red flags or simply was blinded by ambition from seeing them clearly."[16]

These footnotes make clear that the FBI personnel colluded among themselves—ignoring intelligence that established the Steele dossier was fiction in order to press on, gathering FISAs and subpoenaing witnesses, and running informants at campaign insiders suspected of wrongdoing. All these investigatory Hail Marys, like Anthony Ferrante's effort to substantiate Steele's dossier, are nothing more than anti-Trump cabal members trying to save their own necks and fulfill a deep state prayer: bringing down the president.

CHAPTER 5

Obama's Fixer

When you study the output of the Scandal Manufacturers of America's assembly line, certain figures have a way of reappearing, like ghosts who pop up in a never-ending nightmare. Glenn Simpson, as we've seen, is tied to Paul Manafort, Nellie Ohr, Christopher Steele, the DNC via the Perkins Coie law firm, and George Soros's pal, Democracy Integrity Project founder Daniel Jones—and that's just for starters. Stefan Halper is everywhere, too—the guy was an informant for hire and attempted to latch onto Carter Page, George Papadopoulos, and Mike Flynn. But he has connections to foreign intelligence, the CIA, and the FBI.

But one candidate for the most omnipresent government operative in the Trump-Russia scandal universe is a woman who hasn't really been paraded about in the media. She doesn't create headlines; she reacts to them and she makes them go away.

I'm talking about Kathryn "Kathy" Ruemmler, Obama's obstruction angel.

Ruemmler was appointed President Obama's Chief Counsel in June 2011, ascending from her previous year-long role as Principal Deputy Counsel to the President.

To say Obama was a huge fan is an understatement. He called her "an outstanding lawyer with impeccable judgment" and requested she postpone her departure from the White House on three separate occasions. When she finally did leave, he said: "I deeply value her smarts, her judgment, and her wit—but most importantly her uncanny ability to see around the corners that nobody else anticipates."[1]

That "uncanny ability" might be described another way: Ruemmler realized denying media and Congress access to presidential deliberations under the guise of "national security" would help her boss evade scrutiny or calls for accountability for the administration's questionable actions. She didn't need to see around corners if she constructed a policy that kept the president in a cocoon of confidentiality. Obama's legal eagle also navigated the administration through several of its most tawdry scandals, exhibiting several fixer-like skills. She an expert at applying pressure to suppress bad news and she stonewalled like a master mason. These skills, together with her statutory savvy, turned her into a legal human shield for the president.

That cocoon mentality was on full display after Ruemmler got wind of a damning report by the inspector general of the IRS, finding that the nation's tax-collecting agency had improperly targeted the Tea Party and other conservative groups that applied for tax exemption status. Ruemmler huddled with Obama's chief of staff, Denis McDonough, and the decision was made *not to inform the president about a government agency that was harassing his political rivals.*

Shouldn't the president know when major government abuses of power are taking place?

Ruemmler and McDonough decided to keep Obama in the dark because they thought they were protecting him. His ignorance was bliss, they reasoned, because it meant no one could accuse him of trying to influence an investigation![2]

The cone of silence around Obama on this matter blew up before the IG report was finalized, however, when a senior IRS official, Lois Lerner, admitted her organization had conducted special vetting of conservative groups seeking tax-exempt status.[3]

Ruemmler's string-pulling in the wake of the 2012 Secret Service scandal in Cartagena, Colombia, which blazed headlines coast-to-coast when several Secret Service employees hired prostitutes while the president attended an economic summit, is a prime example of her power and questionable scruples. While ten Secret Service agents and ten members of the military lost their jobs after a subsequent investigation, one member of the Obama team, Jonathan Dach, a law student volunteer, who is the son of a Democratic mega-donor and lobbyist, got a free pass in a review of the entourage's actions. According to the *Washington Post*, a log at the Hilton Cartagena Hotel revealed a female guest was registered overnight to Dach's room.

Then-Secret Service Director Mark Sullivan confirmed the finding. Meanwhile, David Nieland, the lead investigator in the Department of Homeland Security inspector general's probe into the debacle said his superiors told him "to withhold and alter certain information in the report of investigation because it was potentially embarrassing to the administration." He also stated he was told "to delay the report of the investigation until after the 2012 election."[4]

Ruemmler ran the White House review of the Cartagena scandal. Her team, predictably, found nothing wrong. Despite the evidence suggesting the volunteer Yale Law School student also sought female companionship, nothing happened. Instead, he was hired as a policy analyst at—surprise!—the State Department in 2014.

Dismissing wrongdoing is one thing, as she apparently did with the Cartagena scandal; it's what defense attorneys are trained to do. But she was the president's attorney; anything that touched or threatened to sully her boss got shut down. Or as the *Washington Post* put it, she was "a fierce opponent of public disclosures that could expose communications within the executive branch, especially those between the president and his advisers." In other words, she wasn't for transparency; she was for turning the Oval Office into a black hole—information could come in; it just could never leave. Transparency, the hallmark of good governance, was anathema to her.

Ruemmler aided and abetted Obama in other ways, too.

In August 2013, following a chemical weapons attack that killed over one thousand people in Damascus, Syria, Obama asked Congress to authorize his use of military force. Failing to amass the needed votes, he did not immediately respond.[5] Ruemmler then helped devise a strategic work-around strategy to justify Obama's ability to order bombings in Syria and neighboring Iraq, citing his commander in chief powers, the 2001 resolution authorizing force against Al Qaeda, and the 2002 resolution authorizing the ouster of Saddam Hussein in Iraq.[6] The moves allowed Obama to set in motion over three thousand airstrikes.

In January 2012, Ruemmler helped sculpt the legal framework that propelled Obama to make a handful of appointments—naming Richard Cordray the director of the Consumer Financial Protection Bureau and anointing three new members to the National Labor Relations Board—during a three-day recess. The move sidestepped the need for congressional approval and the long-standing precedent of only issuing presidential recess appointments during ten-day breaks on Capitol Hill.

After obtaining a memorandum from the Department of Justice that supported her stance, Ruemmler gave an interview framing the question in terms of Senate obstruction. "Can the Senate, through form, render a constitutional power of the executive obsolete?" she asked in order to provide her answer. "Our view is that the answer to that question is clearly no."

THE FIXER IS IN

When she finally left the White House in 2014 to become a partner and global co-chair of the White Collar Defense and Investigations Practice at the vaunted mega law firm Latham & Watkins, she didn't exactly leave the White House behind. In fact, her return to the private sector has been notable for representing scandal-ridden former Obama administration insiders, many of whom were deeply embroiled in the Spygate scandal.

Ruemmler herself has direct ties to Special Counsel Robert Mueller and his so-called investigative dream team dating back to 2007, a moment that represents two high and low points of her career. That year, she worked on the high-profile Merrill Lynch/Enron task force as the number two prosecutor to Andrew Weissmann, the man who would serve a major role as Mueller's primary lieutenant in his hapless collusion investigation. While Ruemmler, who delivered the closing argument against Enron executives Ken Lay and Jeffrey Skilling, helped score convictions for the prosecution, she reportedly hid evidence that would have bolstered the defense's case, possibly exonerating them. The Fifth Circuit reversed twelve out of fourteen counts of conviction in a stunning condemnation of the prosecution.[7]

So much for seeing around corners, right?

One of Ruemmler's clients was her former Obama administration colleague Susan Rice, who served as the president's national security advisor. Rice found herself in the legal hot seat after it was revealed that in 2016 she requested the "unmasking" of names of Trump associates—American citizens—who were mentioned in the classified U.S. intelligence report as the result of surveillance of foreign officials. While there are few restrictions on the CIA and other intelligence agencies probing foreigners, on foreign soil, spying on American citizens is largely against the law without a warrant. When an American is encountered during an operation focused on foreigners, their identity is supposed to be masked.

At the end of Obama's second term, when Brennan, Clapper, and Comey were promoting the debunked, discredited Steele reporting and spreading Glenn Simpson's alarmist whispers, Rice was also rattled by an intelligence report involving members of the Trump transition team. She ordered their names unmasked.

The White House doesn't conduct intelligence investigations, and Rice worked for the White House. So, what was the point of Rice's unmasking request of senior Trump officials? With Ruemmler serving as her lawyer, the story fed to Congress was that Rice was alarmed that the crown prince of the United Arab Emirates, Sheikh Mohammed bin Zayed Al Nahyan, arrived in New York during December 2016, weeks before Trump was sworn into office, without notifying the U.S. government—which is standard protocol. Zayed then met with top Trump officials Jared Kushner, Steve Bannon, and Rice's future replacement, Lieutenant General Michael Flynn. Rice asked for the names of the attendees to be unmasked.

On January 20, 2017—the day of Trump's inauguration—Rice wrote an email and sent it to herself. The email documents a January 5 meeting she attended with President Obama, Joe Biden, Jim Comey, and Deputy Attorney General Sally Yates after an intelligence briefing:

> President Obama began the conversation by stressing his continued commitment to ensuring that every aspect of this issue is handled by the Intelligence and law enforcement communities "by the book". The President stressed that he is not asking about, initiating or instructing anything from a law enforcement perspective. He reiterated that our law enforcement team needs to proceed as it normally would by the book.[8]

But why did Rice bother to request the names? As Andrew McCarthy pointed out in the *National Review*, "if it had been critical to know the identities of Americans caught up in other foreign intelligence efforts, the agencies that collect the information and conduct investigations would have unmasked it."

Seen in this light, going "by the book" would have meant *not unmasking* anyone. Instead, that's exactly what didn't happen. It's also worth asking why the hell Rice was memorializing a two-week-old meeting suddenly, on the last day of her job? Evidently, she got wind there would be questions about the unmasking, and she wanted to cover her ass.

Rice was effectively spying on the incoming administration and attempting to raise flags, as the unmasked report was then distributed to various security agencies. While she may have had the legal right to unmask people—something a Ruemmler-guided figure would make clear—that fact sidesteps whether Rice had abused her power by using that right.

This was pure Ruemmler. Hiding everything under the blanket of executive privilege, insisting that everything was done by the book, even when the outcomes were dubious or horrendous. Yes, Susan Rice could ask for the unmasking. But why didn't she trust the process? Why did she decide the spy agencies, which furnish all manner of intelligence to the president, needed to do better when Trump associates were involved?

The news of the meeting leaked and the names of those in attendance leaked. That's why the unmasking occurred, to feed the onslaught of bogus reports of Team Trump colluding with foreigners.

Ruemmler's post-Obama résumé included another very notable retainer. She became the principal attorney for the Clinton Foundation, according to published reports in 2016. This was not the first time Ruemmler had worked with the Clintons. Early in her career, according to her official career bio, "she served as Associate Counsel to President Bill Clinton where she defended the White House and the Office of the President in independent counsel and congressional investigations."[9] In other words, she represented Bill Clinton when he was caught lying about having sexual relations with Monica Lewinsky. He was not her only client to become embroiled in a tawdry sex scandal.

THE CONSPIRACY CLIENT

Ruemmler has a second Spygate operator on her client list—a guy who is a key player in this prefabricated "collusion" fiasco—and this client was also connected to the meeting that led Susan Rice to ask for the unmasking of the attendees. His name is George Nader, and he is a convicted pedophile.

Born into a Lebanese family, Nader spent his teens in Cleveland, Ohio. As a young man, he launched his own magazine, *Middle East*

Insight, and used it as a vehicle to connect with political figures from the Middle East. Former colleagues describe him as obsessed with contacts and money. But he also had a third fixation: underage sex. He was busted at least twice for importing sex videos and images involving children. Amazingly, because he operated on the fringes of the Swamp where power and access mean so much, he still managed to cling to a career. He got a reduced sentence after one bust when the court was informed that he had worked with Israeli intelligence officers and the leadership of Hezbollah to return hostages to Israel. In 2003, he was convicted on ten charges of sexually abusing children in the Czech Republic and received a one-year prison sentence. Somehow, officials and diplomats still worked with Nader, although there's been speculation his sordid past may actually have appealed to some of the powerful people he worked with.[10]

Nader had a gig advising Sheikh Mohammed bin Zayed of the UAE. In fact, Nader had been at the December meeting attended by Flynn, Kushner, and Bannon that Rice had unmasked. He was also the key figure in a second meeting—the supposedly shocking "back-channel" meeting in the remote Indian Ocean archipelago of Seychelles between bin Zayed, former Blackwater boss and Trump supporter Erik Prince, and Kirill Dmitriev, Putin's Russian banker pal.

We know that years earlier, Nader had worked with Israeli Mossad or Shin Bet agents, because his help was noted in one of his kiddie porn possession trials. We know that he circulated among the Washington, DC, diplomatic community, which was also a fertile hunting ground for spies. Presumably any intel officer worth a damn knew Nader was damaged goods, the perfect "useful idiot" who could be manipulated. His weaknesses made him vulnerable to being exploited.

At some point after his Czech prison sentence, Nader latched onto Blackwater, the private military company. Blackwater is owned by Erik Prince, the son of wealthy, auto-parts manufacturer Edgar Prince, who cofounded the conservative Family Research Council. The Blackwater founder is also the brother of Betsy DeVos, Trump's education secretary, whose husband is the scion of the multibillion-dollar Amway-Alticor fortune, which donates to conservative causes.

I mention all this background detail to put what unfolded into the proper perspective. To recap: an American with a sleazy past, and with contacts in the intelligence community (Nader), went to work for a member of a family that is one of the biggest backers of Trump and the Republican party (Erik Prince) while also working for the leader of the United Arab Emirates (Sheikh Mohammed bin Zayed), who was also employing Blackwater.

Into this mix came Kirill Dmitriev, a Russian who headed his government's sovereign wealth fund and who reported directly to Putin. According to the Mueller Report:

> Dmitriev undertook efforts to meet members of the incoming Trump Administration in the months after the election. Dmitriev asked a close business associate who worked for the United Arab Emirates (UAE) royal court, George Nader, to introduce him to Trump transition officials, and Nader eventually arranged a meeting in the Seychelles between Dmitriev and Erik Prince, a Trump Campaign supporter and an associate of Steve Bannon.[11]

In the many pages of the Mueller Report that focus on the Seychelles meeting, Nader clearly spun that he was reacting to Dmitriev's interest. At one point, in early January, Nader "told Prince that Dmitriev had been pushing Nader to introduce him to someone from the incoming Administration" and "suggested, in light of Prince's relationship with Transition Team officials, that Prince and Dmitriev meet to discuss issues of mutual concern. Prince told Nader that he needed to think further about it and to check with Transition Team officials."

Was this a setup?

It sure sounds like one.

Nader proposed a back channel meeting with a major Putin pal and an associate of senior Trump transition team figures. Prince booked a ticket to Seychelles on January 7, 2017, and Nader arranged for Dmitriev to visit the remote island for a meeting on January 12, 2017. According to the Mueller findings, based on interviews with Nader and Prince, the meeting was a big nothing. "After the Seychelles meetings, Prince told Nader that he would inform Bannon about his discussion with Dmitriev and would convey that someone within the Russian power structure was interested in seeking better relations with the incoming Administration." Prince confirmed this to Mueller's team, telling "the Office that he explained to Bannon that Dmitriev was the head of a Russian sovereign wealth fund and was interested in improving relations between the United States and Russia."[12]

So, what was the point of this meeting?

We know American intelligence was focused on Sheikh bin Zayed. We know that Nader must have appeared on intel radar when he accompanied the Sheikh. We know that Nader's closest relationship with Team Trump was with Prince, who had no formal relationship with the campaign or transition team.

We also know that the FBI had failed to produce any evidence of collusion. Operation Crossfire Hurricane had fizzled out at this point, and Trump was getting ready to claim the Oval Office as Nader was orchestrating this meeting. Who was he working for? Who benefited from a leak of this waste of time?

Once again, we are in the world of optics and illusions. Erik Prince having a meeting with a major Putin money man *looked suspicious*. It fed the collusion narrative illusion. That was its most concrete achievement. At best, it might have provided hard evidence of collusion and, at worst, it provided another angle to foist damaging allegations of impropriety on the Trump administration. And that is exactly what it did, generating pages of conspiracy theories and a lengthy write-up in the Mueller Report designed to play well in the liberal media hit pieces that inevitably followed.

In fact, when news of the Prince/Seychelles meeting first broke, the *Washington Post* reported a spin that portrayed Prince as the one seeking the meeting:

Following the New York meeting between the Emiratis and Trump aides, Zayed was approached by Prince, who said he was authorized to act as an unofficial surrogate for the president-elect, according to the officials. He wanted Zayed to set up a meeting with a Putin associate. Zayed agreed and proposed the Seychelles as the meeting place because of the privacy it would afford both sides. "He wanted to be helpful," one official said of Zayed.[13]

As you can see, this story was a hit job. Just look at the title of the article: "Blackwater Founder Held Secret Seychelles Meeting to Establish Trump-Putin Back Channel." How damning was that? But the Mueller Report repudiated a key element of this story: Nader and Dmitriev drove this meeting. Not Prince. *The Post*'s sources for this inaccurate report remain a mystery. Was it Nader or someone with ties to him? Was it U.S. intelligence or a foreign intelligence source? Either way, their motive seems clear: to make it look like Prince and the Trump team were obsessed with contacting Russia.

Before I move on, I have one more observation: Viewed another way, the entire Seychelles field trip to nowhere actually provides some exculpatory evidence to dismantle the Russia-collusion narrative. If there had been a connection between the Trump campaign and Russia, why, with the inauguration just days away, would there be a mad scramble to make contact through a back channel? This underscores the fact that there wasn't any formal collaboration or coordination. There was no pipeline. If there was, would someone who reported directly to Putin be working feverishly to find a way to make contact? It makes no sense.

THE FIXER'S NEW LOW

George Nader arrived at Washington-Dulles International Airport in January 2018 and was stopped by federal agents working for Mueller's special counsel team. They brandished a warrant related to the collusion investigation that allowed them to seize three iPhones. Searching the phones, investigators uncovered a dozen kiddie porn videos. Nader, who began cooperating with Mueller's team, had reportedly obtained immunity for his work with the special counsel investigation. But that, evidently, did not apply to his possession of illegal sex videos. On June 3, 2019, Nader was finally busted on child porn charges.[14]

Obama's fixer, Kathy Ruemmler, had represented Nader in his dealings with Mueller. According to reports, she remained his lawyer as he faced pedophilia charges. On January 13, 2020, Nader admitted to sex trafficking, pleading guilty to bringing a fourteen-year-old boy to the U.S. for sex. He also admitted to possessing child pornography. A sentencing scheduled for April 10 was delayed, but Nader faces a minimum of ten years in prison and a $250,000 fine. It is not clear if the delay has anything to do with another case Nader faces for conspiring with Lebanese American businessman, Ahmad "Andy" Khawaja, to conceal the source of more than $3.5 million in campaign contributions directed toward Trump and Clinton political action committees.

It is more than a little curious that Kathy Ruemmler represented an operative who appeared to actively engineer a meeting that left the Trump team looking like it was caught in the act of collusion with Russians. It was an outcome that recalled the damaging unmasking performed by Susan Rice. Perhaps she was just drawn to these types of cases.

DEFENDING THE INDEFENSIBLE

America is the biggest victim of the Russiagate debacle. But there are plenty of others. Donald Trump is obviously at the top of the list, as he was the primary target of Glenn Simpson's research, the Steele dossier, and the FBI's subsequent attempts to save itself from itself. But Carter Page, the Trump campaign advisor who was subject to a flood of collusion rumors, was also a major investigative punching bag. The FISA warrant that gave the FBI near-free rein to investigate some campaign operatives from Manafort to Papadopoulos to Flynn and beyond was granted primarily to probe Page. So, it comes as little surprise that in January

2020, Page filed a lawsuit against the Democratic National Committee and Perkins Coie, the law firm that the DNC hired to contract Glenn Simpson and Fusion GPS—who then hired Christopher Steele to write his delusional dossier.

And given the subject of this chapter, it should also come as no surprise that the DNC hired Obama's fixer, Kathy Ruemmler, and other lawyers from her firm to mount its defense. Why would Obama's fixer be the go-to lawyer for a case involving the collusion hoax? She left her White House job in 2014, long before Trump had even announced his candidacy. Would it be because she knew all the players involved? Did she have back channel conversations? Did her client Susan Rice share any other inside information? Or is it because she had sat with George Nader while he was raked over the coals by Robert Mueller, so she knew the ins and outs of Russiagate as well as anyone, if not better?

The lawsuit asserted that the DNC and Perkins Coie misrepresented Page's "connections to and interactions with certain foreign nationals in order to create the false impression that Dr. Page—who served his country honorably in the United States Navy and in the private sector—was in fact an agent of a foreign power, Russia."[15]

Stating "his once-private life" had been destroyed, Page claimed, "The Defendants' wrongful actions convinced many Americans that Dr. Page is a traitor to the United States, and as a result he has received—and continues to receive—multiple death threats."

The strategy to counter Page's lawsuit was classic Ruemmler: don't let facts get in the way of a defense. The legal team challenged Page, saying "the allegedly defamatory statements" against him "were substantially true"—a shocking assertion when you consider how off-the-mark the DNC research provided by Simpson and Steele was. The defense counsel continued:

> Here, the 'gist' of the complained-of statements—that Page coordinated with Russian government contacts as an adviser to the Trump campaign—aligns with Page's own description of his conduct. Page's

own allegations demonstrate the substantial truth of statements that Page traveled to Russia and met with associates of the Russian government. Plaintiffs' defamation claims should be dismissed based on that basis alone.[16]

It will be interesting to see how the Page trial progresses. Inspector General Horowitz's report will provide compelling evidence for the former Trump advisor. As he noted:

> The FBI concluded, among other things, that although consistent with known efforts by Russia to interfere in the 2016 U.S. elections, much of the material in the Steele election reports, including allegations about Donald Trump and members of the Trump campaign relied upon in the Carter Page FISA applications, could not be corroborated; that certain allegations were inaccurate or inconsistent with information gathered by the Crossfire Hurricane team; and that the limited information that was corroborated related to time, location, and title information, much of which was publicly available.[17]

In spring 2020, Kathy Ruemmler signaled she'd had a possible change of heart. Perhaps the voluminous evidence of abuse that Carter Page had gathered awakened her to the damage her clients had wrought by unfurling Russiagate. Or maybe she thought Page might win in court. Or maybe working with the moral vacuum that is George Nader took its toll. It's even possible she realized she'd lost her ability to see around corners and had finally had enough. Or maybe she'd been offered a huge pile of money that she couldn't turn down. Whatever it was, something seemed to have shifted. Obama's fixer signed on to become Global Head of Regulatory Affairs for Goldman Sachs in April 2020. *For now*, it appears Kathy Ruemmler is done cleaning up the Democrats' mess.

CHAPTER 6

The Strange Tale
of Case Agent 1

When the Department of Justice Inspector General Michael Horowitz released his office's 434-page "Review of Four FISA Applications and Other Aspects of the FBI's Crossfire Hurricane investigation" and an accompanying twenty-eight-page executive summary, the world finally got official confirmation of many of the investigatory abuses I've spent years documenting.

I mention this not to crow about being right—I realize saying "I told you so" is annoying—but because the truth is clarifying. The report catalogued the FBI Woods Procedures violations, procedures that were put in place to ensure FISA warrants did not unfairly target U.S. citizens without due cause. Specifically, the application's use of language highlighting Christopher Steele's reliability was called out: "The representations about Steele's prior reporting were overstated and had not been approved by Steele's handling agent, as required by the Woods Procedures."

It also dispelled the FBI's persistent lie that the Steele dossier did not influence its FISA application:

We determined that the Crossfire Hurricane team's receipt of Steele's election reporting on September 19, 2016 played a central and essential role in the FBI's and Department's decision to seek the FISA order.[1]

But there are still things the IG Report left unresolved.

CHAOS AGENT

Horowitz's massive investigation mentions a huge cast of characters. James Comey is mentioned 148 times. Joseph Mifsud, the Maltese man of mystery who George Papadopoulos says first mentioned that the Russians had material that would hurt Hillary Clinton, is mentioned 40 times. Fusion GPS is named 139 times. Counterintelligence Division Assistant Director William "Bill" Priestap is mentioned 165 times.

And someone named Special Agent 1 is cited 231 times. That averages out to more than one appearance every other page.

The *New York Times* identified Special Agent 1 as Stephen M. Somma, a former counterintelligence investigator in the FBI's New York field office who had been transferred to Washington to work on the spying operation on the Trump team, code-named Crossfire Hurricane.[2]

Why is Somma—or his alias "Special Agent 1"—mentioned so many times in the report? The short version is that he appears to be the agent who bent, twisted, and ignored agency protocol to get a warrant to spy on Trump team member Carter Page, which allowed the FBI to widen the scope of its investigation into the Trump campaign.

Or as the inspector general put it: "Case Agent 1 was primarily responsible for some of the most significant errors and omissions in the FISA applications."[3]

But exactly why Agent Somma was in the position he was in, why he aggressively pushed the storylines he did, and how and when he found out about those storylines—especially the Steele dossier itself—remain puzzling questions. These mysteries shed light on just how out of control things were as the rush to confirm the fabricated collusion hoax and to nail Trump took hold of the Russiagate investigators.

Stephen Somma was very much at the center of this chaos.

INSIDE INFORMATION

To understand the level of underhandedness going on, let's go back to the beginning of Crossfire Hurricane. The investigation was allegedly opened on July 31 (I write "allegedly" because although July 31 is the date of the administrative opening of the Crossfire Hurricane case, there is significant evidence that the investigation began much earlier—including the July 5, 2016, meeting between FBI agent Gaeta and Steele). This was five days after a "Friendly Foreign Source"—Australia—informed the FBI that Trump campaign foreign policy advisor George Papadopoulos indicated the Trump team had "received some kind of suggestion from Russia" regarding the anonymous release of information during the campaign that would be damaging to Clinton.[4]

According to this plotline, Papadopoulos, the subject of the "tip," should have been the focal point of the investigation. Instead, we know that Agent Somma instantly pushed to obtain a FISA warrant on Carter Page, not Papadopoulos. Here's the IG Report:

> **Almost immediately after opening the Page, Papadopoulos, and Manafort investigations on August 10, the case agent assigned to the Carter Page investigation, Case Agent 1, contacted the OGC [the FBI's Office of General Counsel] about the possibility of seeking FISA authority for Carter Page.**

The IG says the investigative team concluded that Page's "prior contacts with known Russian intelligence officers...made him most receptive to receiving the offer of assistance from the Russians reported in the FFG information." Somma then claimed that a warrant on Page allowing electronic surveillance of emails and other communications "would help provide valuable information about what Page did while in Moscow in July 2016 and the Russian officials with whom he may have spoken."[5]

That explanation sounds reasonable at first. But when you parse it, you will realize this is either remarkably disingenuous spin or really poor intelligence analysis. Several other Trump campaign team members had contacts with Russian operatives. In fact, you could argue that if you dig hard enough, all the senior movers and shakers on Capitol Hill, and from the Obama administration as well, had some tangential contact with Russians. As a reminder to the media hacks who feigned confusion about this point, contact with Russian individuals is not illegal; *illegal contact with Russians is illegal.* I don't want to needlessly cast undeserving aspersions on other Trump team members, but there were obviously other Trump team members who could've been tarred and feathered with the nonsense labels the Spygate conspirators used based on the same loose, "receptive" category per the FBI's broad definition of "collusion." So Somma's reason for targeting Page seems flimsy, and such ridiculous criteria could be used to target nearly every member of Congress.

Anyone who scrutinizes the timing of Somma's conclusions is likely to smell a rat. Let me back up again: Somma was a Russian ops expert when he worked in the New York FBI field office. *The Federalist* reports that before Somma came to DC to join the Operation Crossfire team in August, he worked as a special agent in counterintelligence in New York where he zeroed in on Russian operations. That suggests he was operational in the New York office around the time Steele's Rome-based handler, FBI agent Michael Gaeta, sent a copy of Steele's first two memos to an FBI supervisor in the New York office on July 28.[6] The earliest dated memo was from June 20, 2016. Date-wise, it was followed by one from July 19, which was titled "Russia: Secret Kremlin Meetings Attended by Trump Advisor, Carter Page in Moscow." The logic behind the sequencing of Steele's dossier remains a mystery; the July 19 memo is numbered 094, the July 30 memo is numbered 097, while another document dated July 26 is numbered 086. But we know, per the IG report, that Handling Agent 1 (Gaeta) sent Reports 80 and 94 to the New York field office.[7] We're also reasonably confident, based on the testimony of FBI lawyer Lisa Page, that Steele's memo number 095—which was suspiciously undated, and which expounds on the nonsensical Carter Page collusion nonsense—likely arrived on July 28, *the same day* the memos arrived in the New York field office from Steele's FBI handler Gaeta. In an exchange with former GOP congressman Trey Gowdy, Lisa Page was asked about the formal opening of the Crossfire Hurricane case at the end of July.

"You learned about it on the 28th?" Gowdy said.

"Right, thank you," Page said.

Yet, FBI brass continue to stick to their absurd narrative that the Australian Downer/Papadopoulos tip was the reason they opened the case against the Trump team, rather than the Steele dossier memos that arrived in the New York office from Gaeta, and the DC headquarters team Lisa Page was part of, on July 28, just three days before the formal opening of the case.

The Federalist also reports that the assistant special agent in charge at the New York office reportedly told Gaeta the memos would be "walled off" from other agents in the office. But if Russiagate has taught us anything, it's that some law enforcement and government agencies leak worse than the *Titanic*. In fact, given their agendas, some of these agencies don't just suffer from small leaks, they often spew like fountains. Three days after the formal case opening, on August 3, the Steele memos were discussed at a meeting between the assistant special agent in charge, a supervisory special agent, and two FBI lawyers. And just like that, Carter Page was now on the radar of four FBI officials in the U.S.[8]

It took six weeks before the Crossfire Hurricane team—allegedly—received Steele's full dossier, on September 19, 2016. According to the IG findings, that dossier played a central and essential role in the FBI's and Justice Department's decision to seek the FISA order.

But as we've already noted, Somma was pushing for a FISA in early August. Why?

Specifically, what did Somma know about Carter Page on August 10?

Did Somma, who worked the Russia desk, learn of Steele's report in late July, as Lisa Page did, or in early August, before the memos made their way to DC?

If Somma had heard about Steele's whispers of collusion, perhaps that helped shape his push to target Carter Page for a FISA warrant. But if he had learned about it earlier, then the FBI's story that the dossier memo about Page didn't cause them to open the case would be proven false. Again, the IG report provides a timeline revealing Somma's gung ho focus on Carter Page.

Maybe he had also learned of Carter Page from other FBI sources. Did he know about the January 23, 2015, sealed complaint sworn to by FBI agent Gregory Monaghan and filed in the Southern District of New York against three agents of Russia's Foreign Intelligence Service (SVR), Evgeny Buryakov, Igor Sporyshev, and Victor Podobnyy? That complaint revealed the three Russians discussed efforts to target Page in April 2013 and turn him into an "intelligence source." It seems likely Somma actually knew or knew of Gregory Monaghan since they both worked on Russian intelligence in New York.[9]

Or maybe, just maybe, his pals in the New York office told him about Steele's report.

In other words, Somma may have had more information on Crossfire Hurricane targets than any of his colleagues.

I want to reiterate just how in the dark the FBI investigators were after hearing Alexander Downer's version of what George Papadopoulos told him. Here is Bill Priestap describing how the investigators were flying blind ("FFG" stands for Friendly Foreign Government, in this case, Australia):

> **In regard to the information the [FFG] provided us, we had no indication as to which person in the Trump campaign allegedly received**

the offer from the Russians. There was no specific U.S. person identified. We also had no indication, whatsoever, that the person affiliated with the Trump campaign had rejected the alleged offer from the Russians. In fact, the information we received indicated that Papadopoulos told the [FFG] he felt confident Mr. Trump would win the election, and Papadopoulos commented that the Clintons had a lot of baggage and that the Trump team had plenty of material to use in its campaign. While Papadopoulos didn't say where the Trump team had received the "material," one could reasonably infer that some of the material might have come from the Russians.[10]

The IG report tells us that when the Crossfire Hurricane team finally "received Steele's election reporting on September 19, 2016," the dossier "played a central and essential role in the FBI's and Department's decision to seek the FISA order." This means that although the investigators literally had no clue who the Russians might have contacted, Somma had zeroed in on Carter Page *at least nine days before* his team allegedly received Steele's reports alleging Carter Page of having a "secret meeting" with Putin "close associate and US-sanctioned individual, Igor SECHIN."

Given all these facts and circumstances, it's hard to understand how the IG didn't at least mention investigating the timeline with regard to Somma. It seems very likely he was operating on inside information.

The IG did devote a scathing appraisal to Somma's job performance in the investigation, saddling him with the most egregious FISA errors, including failures to accurately relay and update information. Here is the full damning summation:

> As noted throughout this report, Case Agent 1 was primarily responsible for some of the most significant errors and omissions in the FISA applications, including (1) the mischaracterization of Steele's prior reporting resulting from his failure to seek review and approval of the statement from the handling agent, as the Woods Procedures required, (2) the failure to advise [the National Security Division's

Office of Intelligence] of Papadopoulos's statements to FBI [Confidential Human Sources] that were inconsistent with the Steele reporting relied upon in the FISA applications that there was a "well-developed conspiracy of cooperation" between individuals associated with the Trump campaign and Russia, (3) the failure to advise [Office of Intelligence] of Page's statements to an FBI [Confidential Human Source] regarding him having no communications with Manafort and denying the alleged meetings with Sechin and Divyekin, (4) providing inaccurate and incomplete information to 01 about information provided by another U.S. government agency regarding its past relationship with Page that was highly relevant to the applications, (5) the failure to advise [the Office of Intelligence] of the information from Bruce Ohr about Steele and his election reporting, and (6) the failure to advise 01 of the inconsistences [sic] between Steele and his Primary Sub-source. The explanations that Case Agent 1 provided for these errors and omissions are summarized in Chapter Five and Chapter Eight of this report. While we found no documentary or testimonial evidence that this pattern of errors by Case Agent 1 was intentional, we also did not find his explanations for so many significant and repeated failures to be satisfactory. We therefore concluded that these explanations did not excuse his failure to meet his responsibility to ensure that the initial FISA application, the first renewal application, and the third renewal application were "scrupulously accurate."[11]

As poor a performer as Somma was, he was not alone. The buck should have stopped with him. Instead, it got passed up through the chain of command at the bureau—to Priestap, Strzok, McCabe, and Comey, and then to Rod Rosenstein, who appointed Robert Mueller special counsel. All of them should have asked questions and pushed Somma to clarify the fast-and-loose assertions made in the FISA application. The IG report reaffirms this, noting, "We similarly found errors by supervisory FBI employees with responsibility for the accuracy of the FBI applications."[12]

SOMMA'S "HUMAN CONFIDENTIAL SOURCE"

There is another angle to Crossfire Hurricane that is cause for grave concern regarding Stephen Somma. He was the agent who had previously handled Stefan Halper—the man cloaked in the IG report as "Source 2." Details about the "pre-existing" relationship between the agent and the informant remain murky. But Somma claimed he reached out to Halper for guidance and perspective—he had never worked on an investigation that involved political campaigns and felt he lacked insight and understanding of basic campaign roles. So why turn to Halper? "Case Agent 1 knew that Source 2 had been affiliated with national political campaigns since the early 1970s" explains the report.[13]

Did you just choke on that last sentence? I did. The difference between a 1970s campaign and a modern campaign is night and day. Sure, the goal remains the same—raise money, campaign, win. But give me a break. There was no internet or social media in 1970. Campaign finance and fundraising were vastly different. Polling was more primitive. The Cold War dictated geopolitical policy. It seemed absurd that Somma would turn to a political dinosaur like Halper, now seventy-five, who hadn't been involved in presidential politics since the Reagan administration.

But then, Halper was a master of dirty campaign tricks. In 1983, the *New York Times* reported that Halper, while working on Reagan's 1980 presidential campaign, headed an operation to gather inside information on the Carter administration's foreign policy plans.[14] So maybe there was a method to Somma's madness in this regard. He knew something about opposition research.

On August 11, Somma, a fellow case agent, and Halper met, joined by a member of the FBI support staff. The agents asked Halper about George Papadopoulos. Halper said he had never heard of the Trump advisor. Then he did something incredible. Out of nowhere, he "asked whether the team had any interest in an individual named Carter Page." Somma said the agents asked how Halper knew Carter Page and were informed that just one month earlier, in mid-July 2016, Page attended a three-day conference that Halper was involved in and actually asked Halper to be a foreign policy advisor for the Trump campaign.[15]

Imagine that!

Somma ran Halper as a source. Somma mentioned on August 10 that a FISA warrant on Carter Page would be advisable. And then, *the next day*, Halper showed up to a meeting with Somma and another case agent and—apparently totally out of the blue—asked if they had any interest in Carter Page because Page had tried to recruit him. Not only that, but Halper said he "was expecting to be contacted in the near future by one of the senior leaders of the Trump campaign about joining the campaign."[16]

It's like a dream come true, right? Somma must have been saying, "Somebody, pinch me!"

Either that or: "Is anyone buying this? Are we going to get busted?"

Halper wasn't done, however. He also spilled that he had known Trump's then-campaign manager, Manafort, for a number of years and that he had been previously acquainted with Michael Flynn.

Despite having handled Halper previously, Somma claimed all of Halper's connections with the targets of the Crossfire Hurricane investigation were unknown to him. In his words, Halper's connections were "serendipitous." He told IG investigators, "Quite honestly…we kind of stumbled upon Halper knowing these folks."

What did the rest of the Crossfire Hurricane team think about this? They "couldn't believe [their] luck," Somma said.[17]

Frankly, neither can I. The entire setup strains credulity, and I'm being polite. It's total BS.

We now know another source who says that Halper was lying to the FBI: Carter Page himself. Page told ace reporter Margot Cleveland that he and Halper attended a dinner at Magdalene College in Cambridge, England, hosted by former Anglican Archbishop Rowan Williams on Sunday, July 10, 2016. "It was a small dinner with only about a dozen or so people in attendance…pretty much everyone got to meet and speak with everyone," Page said. So much for Halper's spin implying Page had sought him out.

Page also denied asking Halper to join the Trump campaign—as if he even had the power to authorize such a role without Trump campaign national co-chair Sam Clovis's input. "That is quite clearly not a correct characterization. I never asked him 'to be a foreign policy advisor for the Trump campaign,'" Page said, admitting they might have discussed ways Halper might one day work with the campaign.[18]

Halper's presence at the Cambridge event, "2016's Race to Change the World," which was hosted by the Centre for Research in the Arts, Social Sciences and Humanities, makes sense. Halper, a professor at Cambridge's Department of Politics and International Studies, spoke at the event, and his department, which is located in the same building that houses the Centre for Research, reportedly supported the event.

How Page wound up there—with organizers paying his round-trip fare to the event—remains something of a mystery. According to the *Wall Street Journal*, the invitation to the event came at the end of May or early June, but Page declined to say who sent the invitation, although he says it was not Halper.[19]

This sequence of events is truly fascinating. And it reeks of a setup. Just look at the timing. On March 21, Trump gave an interview naming five foreign policy advisors, including Carter Page and George Papadopoulos. These guys were bit players who had never had such high-profile gigs in their lives. That made them ideal targets for intelligence operations.

Sure enough, Papadopoulos was contacted by the mysterious Joseph Mifsud, who by April 2016 allegedly spun tales of Russian interference. And then two months later, Carter Page got an expenses-paid invite and ended up eating dinner with Halper, a former CIA asset with a long history of spycraft, political sabotage, and intelligence connections.

Halper is also close with Sir Richard Dearlove, the former head of England's MI6, who, as I noted elsewhere, worked previously with

Christopher Steele. It's anyone's guess how many other former MI6 operatives Halper knew. Cambridge has long been a famous stomping ground for recruiting intelligence assets, including the infamous Cambridge Four, a group of students at Trinity Hall who became moles for the Soviet Union. So it seems more than likely that Halper, an ex-CIA asset whose father-in-law was former CIA Deputy Director Ray Cline[20] and who once listed First Deputy of the Foreign Minister for Russia Vyacheslav Trubnikov as an advisor to a research paper he wrote for the Department of Defense,[21] had plenty of contacts. Is it possible any of them fed Halper Carter Page's name and suggested the rookie Trump advisor might be someone worth targeting?

It sure seems that way.

Only eight days after Page met with Halper, Christopher Steele wrote his July 19 memo detailing Page's supposed meeting with Rosneft. Is it possible that Halper, given his indirect connections to Steele, might have fed the anti-Trump Orbis operative information on Page?

It sure seems that way.

Is it possible that Halper, having somehow wagged Steele, then told his handler Somma about Page, too? Is it possible that a veteran counterintelligence agent like Somma was played and spun by Halper? And that Halper, having duped Somma, also played and spun the rest of Operation Crossfire Hurricane?

It sure seems that way.

Or is it possible Somma and Halper coordinated the entire Page angle because Somma, a Russian counterintelligence agent for the FBI, already knew Page had been targeted by Russian spies? So, in fact, Somma might have been driving Halper?

That seems very possible, too.

I'm not the only one who has been asking these questions. Margot Cleveland wrote: "The evidence strongly suggests someone charged Halper with contacting Page in mid-July, raising several questions: Was Halper a source for the CIA, or another intelligence agency? Or was Halper a source for Steele? And did Somma know of Halper's meeting with Page before arranging for him to talk with the Crossfire Hurricane team?"[22]

Unfortunately, the IG seems to have accepted Somma and Halper's ridiculous "It was serendipity!" explanation. Coincidence is certainly one potentially valid interpretation of events. Incompetence is another. But there are simply too many coincidences and too much incompetence to write off this chain of events as a series of highly unlikely meetings and extremely careless decisions.

Halper, as we'll see in the next chapter, has a history of using Cambridge dinners to make trouble. Two years earlier, in 2014, while at an event called the Cambridge Intelligence Seminar, his pal Dearlove dined with then-Defense Intelligence Agency Director Michael Flynn. That dinner kicked off a smear campaign that is still unfolding. It would be interesting to know what Stephen Somma knew about Halper's involvement in that operation.

But Somma isn't talking.

And given all that has unfolded in this travesty of investigatory abuse and incompetence, can you blame him? I'd disappear, too.

CHAPTER 7

The Attempted Destruction of General Mike Flynn

O f all the charges leveled by the FBI and Mueller investigative team, none is sleazier than the prosecution—or should I say persecution—of Lieutenant General Michael Flynn, President Trump's former national security advisor.

And while we're cataloging the abuse he's suffered, none is more underhanded, unfounded, and undeserved.

On December 1, 2017, Flynn pleaded guilty to lying to the FBI about conversations with then-Russian ambassador to the U.S. Sergey Kislyak that took place on December 29, 2016. It was a big deal in the entire Russiagate fiasco for a number of reasons. Flynn was a high-profile member of the Trump administration—a valued campaign team member who had been active with the campaign for months. It would also be the first conviction of a Trump associate by the Mueller team. From a public relations point of view, it could be used to justify the absurd witch hunt that was the entire Russiagate investigation.

The Mueller team's PR logic was swallowed like candy by the mainstream media: If Flynn was "lying," then he must be "hiding something."

And if one Trump associate was "hiding something," then there must be something nefarious and sinister going on in the Trump orbit. Cue the chorus of C-words! Conspiracy and collusion! Fire up the scandal manufacturing assembly line. This was the narrative needed to justify the Department of Justice's Rod Rosenstein and Special Counsel Robert Mueller's multimillion-dollar fishing expedition to find fault with the Trump campaign, to justify the Mueller probe's existence, and to save the reputation of the FBI.

Ironically, there is plenty of evidence to suggest there was a conspiracy, but it had nothing to do with Flynn. If anything, Flynn was the target and victim of an elaborately orchestrated prosecution hit, not the perpetrator.

The evidence supporting Flynn, which has leaked out over a period of more than four years, suggests that intelligence operatives have been fixated on the retired three-star general, both fabricating flimsy charges against him and suppressing evidence that would exonerate him.

To fully explain all this, I'm going to dig into three separate plotlines, some with ties to the FBI and the intelligence community swamp. These tales involve Russians. But they also involve U.S. intelligence operatives and hostile tactics of senior government officials, not to mention covert operations and selective spin designed to damage Flynn's reputation. Why? Because General Flynn was an experienced intelligence professional who had a history of calling for reforms to the entrenched intelligence bureaucracy and because, as Trump's national security advisor, he was about to uncover the plot against the Trump team.

THE BACK STORY

Before I get to the unprecedented takedown of Mike Flynn, I want to share why he was targeted on three separate occasions. What did Flynn do to earn the wrath of so many in the intelligence community?

In 2009, Flynn, who had distinguished himself as the chief intelligence officer for Joint Special Operations Command in Iraq, was named the intel chief in Afghanistan under General Stanley McChrystal. Tough-talking McChrystal asked Flynn to write up an assessment of U.S. involvement in the country, where U.S. forces had been hunkered down for eight years. Flynn embraced his Afghanistan-intel evaluation with gusto. The results caused, in the words of columnist Max Boot, "a minor earthquake in the Pentagon." But that's an understatement—his analysis also sent reverberations to the CIA headquarters in Langley, Virginia. Instead of sharing the report up the chain of command where it might have been watered down or buried within the Department of Defense's bureaucracy, Flynn sidestepped the process and released his damning article via a Washington think-tank called Center for a New American Security.[1]

Here's his opening salvo:

> Eight years into the war in Afghanistan, the U.S. intelligence community is only marginally relevant to the overall strategy. Having focused the overwhelming majority of its collection efforts and analytical brainpower on insurgent groups, the vast intelligence apparatus is unable to answer fundamental questions about the environment in which U.S. and allied forces operate and the people they seek to persuade. Ignorant of local economics and landowners, hazy about who the powerbrokers are and how they might be influenced, incurious about the correlations between various development projects and the levels of cooperation among villagers, and disengaged from people in the best position to find answers—whether aid workers or Afghan soldiers—U.S. intelligence officers and analysts can do little but shrug in response to high level decision-makers seeking the knowledge, analysis, and information they need to wage a successful counterinsurgency.[2]

In one sense, this report put Flynn on the map. He was speaking the truth, as he saw it. And he would continue his rise within the Department of Defense, eventually becoming the director of the Defense Intelligence Agency, a seventeen-thousand-member intelligence operation. Based on simple risk-rewards arithmetic, you can see how he might think that being outspoken wasn't a bad thing.

In another sense, the report helped seal his fate.

It did this by calling out other intelligence programs—remember the CIA had been in Afghanistan and Pakistan for decades. The agency thought up Operation Cyclone, which gave arms and funds to Islamist mujahideen members to battle the Soviet Union in the 1980s. And then, having helped give rise to the Taliban, the CIA was instrumental in calling the shots when it came to targeting Al Qaeda. So, Mike Flynn made an untold number of enemies within the CIA with his appraisal. He had called them "marginally relevant," "ignorant," and unable to provide the "knowledge, analysis, and information" needed "to wage a successful counterinsurgency."

It was a brutal assessment.

Flynn's blunt manner and maverick perspectives also worked against him in the long run. During his time in Iraq and Afghanistan, he became convinced that the U.S. policy of taking out terrorist leaders was an ineffective way to win the war on terror. It was a losing battle, he reasoned. There was always another bloodthirsty demagogue waiting to wage war against us. Meanwhile, intelligence reports he saw indicated that radical Islamist terrorist threats were increasing, not decreasing, as the Obama administration seemed to think. He began to believe that national intelligence was being subjected to undue political influence; it was being cherry-picked and sliced and diced to paint a misleading positive picture.

"I read the Presidential Daily Briefs and the minutes of the National Security Council's deputies meetings, and it was very, very clear to me that reporting on the terrorism threat that came up the intelligence community's chain of command was very different from what was being presented at the top levels of government," Flynn told James Kitfield in a *Politico* article. "That intelligence made it very clear that Al Qaeda and its affiliates were not on the run, but were instead rapidly expanding. The number of terrorist attacks was on the rise, and Iraq was starting to burn again. So that was Obama's big lie—that the enemy was on the run, and we were beating these guys."[3]

Flynn began to advocate for a more comprehensive approach to regime change in the Middle East. In his book *The Field of Fight: How We Can Win the Global War Against Radical Islam and Its Allies*, he writes, "We can't win this war by treating radical Islamic terrorists as a handful of crazies. The political and theological underpinnings of their immoral actions have to be demolished."[4] This out-of-the-box thinking alienated many in the politically correct Obama administration, and Flynn became a pariah within the Obama-sphere; he was forcibly retired in 2014 by Obama, reportedly at the urging of National Intelligence Director James Clapper and Michael Vickers, the undersecretary of defense for intelligence. Flynn left the armed forces in a ceremony that featured Admiral Mike Rogers, the director of the National Security Agency, calling him "the best intelligence officer of the past 20 years."[5]

After thirty-three years of service to his country, powerful members of his country were about to do an unconscionable disservice to him.

THE FIRST SETUP

On May 24, 2019, a Russian-born, UK citizen named Svetlana Lokhova filed a lawsuit in federal court alleging defamation and seeking $25,350,000 in damages from five defendants. The first one named in the action was the central player in the last chapter, Stefan Halper, the FBI informant who heavily influenced the Crossfire Hurricane investigation into the Trump team. The first paragraph in the introduction of the sixty-six-page filing doesn't mince words:

> 1. Stefan Halper is a ratf**ker and a spy, who embroiled an innocent woman in a conspiracy to undo the 2016 Presidential election and topple the President of the United States of America.[6]

Lokhova wasn't the only victim. In fact, she was what intelligence agents might consider "collateral damage"—a demeaning term for a mother of a small child embroiled, unwillingly, in an international scandal and who had her life nearly destroyed by a whisper campaign that sought to tie her to a nefarious spy operation.

And what was that operation?

Some readers may be familiar with Lokhova, but it is worth revisiting her story and her lawsuit because it reveals just how sleazy the first setup of Michael Flynn was.

In February 2014, Flynn was in his second year as the director of the DIA when he crossed paths with Lokhova, an academic who had done postgraduate work at Cambridge. Both Flynn and Lokhova had been invited to a dinner reportedly partially organized by Stefan Halper. (Yes, Halper apparently had established dinner parties as a tool to compromise targets long before Carter Page ambled into view.) At the dinner were Halper's associates Sir Richard Dearlove, the former MI6 chief, and Christopher Andrew, a Cambridge professor, an MI5 historian who had taught Lokhova. This trio of intelligence "experts" was running the Cambridge Intelligence Seminar, a kind of Spies 'R' Us convention for members of the intelligence community. It's important to note here that, according to Lokhova, Halper was not at the dinner, and no photographic evidence has ever surfaced placing Halper at the event. This is critical given the FBI's use of an informant, believed to be Halper, who stated to the FBI that he witnessed suspicious behavior between Flynn and Lokhova at the dinner.

Flynn showed up to the dinner with a DIA coworker named Dan O'Brien, who headed the DIA's liaison office in London. The dinner was a fairly large affair. O'Brien said there were around twenty graduate students there and that Flynn's behavior or interactions were unremarkable. "Nothing rose to the level" that would have raised any concerns of impropriety, he told the *Wall Street Journal*.[7]

Flynn did, in fact, cross paths with Lokhova. According to her boyfriend David North, Flynn and Lokhova "had a 20-minute public conversation." North, who picked Lokhova up after the dinner—alone—said Flynn has "not met or spoke since" with Lokhova.[8]

An FBI draft document dated January 4, 2017, that was prepared to close the agency's investigation on Flynn reveals that "an established" confidential human source (CHS) told agents he had seen Lokhova and Flynn at the dinner. Here's how the FBI summarized the CHS—who was, presumably, Halper. Crossfire Razor is the code name the FBI assigned to Flynn:

> During the debriefing, the CHS relayed an incident s/he witnessed when CROSSFIRE RAZOR (CR) spoke at the [Redacted] in [Redacted]. The CHS was unsure of the date, but noted that CROSS-FIRE RAZOR was still in his/her position within the [US Intelligence Community]…. The CHS advised that after CR spoke and socialized with members of [Redacted] at dinner and over drinks, members of [Redacted] got CR a cab to the train station…. The CHS stated that a [Redacted] surprised everyone and got into CR's cab and joined CR on the train ride to [Redacted].[9]

Unless the FBI had interviewed another "established" source with ties to Cambridge, Halper is indeed the confidential human source recounting that tale. But if Lokhova is correct and Halper was not in attendance—something Lokhova swore up and down to me in an interview—then Halper was lying to the FBI. His shocking claim that he saw Lokhova get in the cab with Flynn is a complete fabrication for two very good reasons: 1) Halper wasn't at the party and 2) *it didn't happen.*

The irony here is painful. As we shall see, Flynn was eventually threatened with the charge of lying to the FBI. Stefan Halper? He got a check from the U.S. government for what appears to be his "creative" services.

In interviews, Lokhova has called Halper's offensive "a textbook 'black-op' to dirty up the reputation of a political opponent. He needed an innocuous social event to place Flynn in a room with a woman who was ethnically Russian." Having achieved that, Halper stowed this meeting away in his files. The proximity of Flynn and Lokhova at the dinner

party was an innocent fact that could be weaponized later to cripple
Flynn—the intelligence officer who had dared criticize the CIA, and
other intel agencies.

To understand the full impact of the activities surrounding
Halper—the elaborate timing and orchestration to feed the illusion of
a conspiracy—we need to put this setup aside for a moment. When
intelligence agents set up an operation and then sit back and wait to
activate it, it's likely a sleeper operation. And that, in a sense, was what
the Cambridge dinner was.

THE SECOND SETUP

Michael Flynn began associating with the Trump campaign in February
2016. By the time Trump won the Republican presidential nomination,
Flynn was a force to be reckoned with, appearing on stage at the Republican National Convention to endorse Trump and then joining the crowd
with "Lock her up!" chants aimed at Hillary Clinton. "Lock her up! Lock
her up! Damn right! Exactly right!" Flynn urged the crowd. "There is
nothing wrong with that!"[10]

After Trump's shocking upset victory, the president-elect chose
General Flynn as his national security advisor. Taking a break from the
transition team planning, Flynn and his wife flew to the Dominican
Republic for a brief vacation after Christmas. Meanwhile, on December
28, President Barack Obama finally took action, which, he alleged, was
to punish Russia for interference with the 2016 presidential election,
signing Executive Order 13757 that detailed sanctions against Russia
and included the expulsion of thirty-five Russian diplomats from the
United States.

I want to stress the timing of this event. The evidence against Russia
had been accumulating since June with regard to the alleged Russian
hack of the Democratic National Committee and the subsequent dump
of the DNC's emails to Wikileaks. On October 7, 2016, the Department of Homeland Security and Office of the Director of National

Intelligence on Election Security issued a joint statement: "The U.S. Intelligence Community (USIC) is confident that the Russian Government directed the recent compromises of e-mails from US persons and institutions, including from US political organizations. The recent disclosures of alleged hacked e-mails on sites like DCLeaks.com and WikiLeaks and by the Guccifer 2.0 online persona are consistent with the methods and motivations of Russian-directed efforts. These thefts and disclosures are intended to interfere with the US election process."[11]

Why did President Obama wait so long—nearly three months—to fire back at Putin? Was he scared of inflaming Putin and having Russia sow more chaos? Or, more likely, was he waiting in case Trump won the presidency and he needed to discredit the shocking political election victory of Donald Trump?

The administration expected the announcement of the expulsion of the Russian diplomats would set off a crisis. Gaming out the possible reactions, intelligence strategists must have anticipated a number of responses, including the idea that the Russians would likely reach out to the incoming Trump administration and their national security team. That, in turn, might result in the violation of a little-known, never-successfully-prosecuted law known as the Logan Act. This likely unconstitutional law, passed in 1799, forbids U.S. citizens from carrying "on any correspondence or intercourse with any foreign government or any officer or agent thereof, in relation to any disputes or controversies with the United States, or to defeat the measures of the United States." It has been used exactly once in over 220 years to hand down an indictment.[12]

But if the Russians did reach out to someone in the incoming administration, how would law enforcement know? They couldn't monitor the Trump team without a warrant. These were American citizens, after all.

But the FBI got lucky.

Or maybe it wasn't luck.

As a matter of course—and national security—the intelligence community monitored calls from Russian Ambassador Kislyak.

And on the day the sanctions against Russia were announced, Michael Flynn, the president-elect's incoming national security advisor, received a text from then-Russian ambassador Sergey Kislyak, according to the FBI. It said: "Can you call me?"

Flynn said he didn't see the text until the next day, which is understandable. *He was on vacation.* When he did see it, he texted back, saying he could talk in fifteen to twenty minutes.

Remember—and this is very important—that before this moment, Flynn was relaxing and unplugging from the world. This has been known to happen at beach resorts in the Dominican Republic; it's not mysterious what people do on *vacation*. You might even say, that's the whole purpose of vacationers going to the DR. So, it's possible, and even likely, that Flynn wasn't even aware of all the fine details of Obama's expulsion of the Russians when he read Kislyak's text.

Flynn then called KT McFarland, the incoming deputy national security advisor who was at Mar-a-Lago with other members of the Trump transition team, to discuss messaging to Kislyak. This seems like responsible behavior for an incoming administration that is going to function in the real world, in real-time.

According to court records filed by Robert Mueller's prosecution team, that call was monitored. In it, Flynn and McFarland "discussed the U.S. sanctions, including the potential impact of those sanctions on the incoming administration's foreign policy goals," according to the filing. Additionally, McFarland relayed that Trump team members "did not want Russia to escalate the situation."[13]

Flynn called Kislyak. During the exchange, which was also monitored, Flynn "requested that Russia not escalate the situation and only respond to the U.S. sanctions in a reciprocal manner."[14]

Then, on December 30, 2016, Vladimir Putin issued a statement indicating that Russia would not respond with retaliatory measures over the sanctions.

I've already mentioned that the FBI was monitoring Kislyak's calls. But who, why, and how were Flynn's calls to KT McFarland monitored?

There have been several theories. One was that Flynn was a target of a separate monitoring operation, and the FBI was monitoring his phone. Another was that Flynn's location lacked a sensitive compartmented information facility to ensure a secure communications channel. That may have exposed his calls to other intelligence agencies, including some who work closely with the CIA. As I explained at the opening of the chapter, the CIA was not filled with Mike Flynn fans. Did they get a hold of these calls and share them?

The FBI and the Mueller team alleged the calls were documented in intelligence reports and that Flynn's name was reported. The U.S. Foreign Intelligence Surveillance Act (FISA) generally requires that the identity of Americans caught in surveillance operations must be "masked," or hidden, when reports are filed. That means they are identified in broad, nonspecific terms, like "Administration Member 1."

So why was Flynn named?

As Acting Attorney General Sally Yates—who figures heavily in the finale of the Flynn takedown—later explained, Flynn's name was never "unmasked" because it had never actually been masked. Minimization requirements can be ignored, she said, when "intelligence only made sense if you knew who the identity of the U.S. person was." The other exception, she added, is "if it's evidence of a crime."[15]

Everyone understand this bizarre logic? Because Flynn, by doing his job as the incoming national security advisor and talking to Ambassador Kislyak, might have been violating a ridiculous law which no one has ever been prosecuted for, and because anyone reading the intelligence report would fail to understand the importance of Flynn talking to the Russian ambassador (thereby possibly violating the law that no one has ever been prosecuted for) without identifying him, it was perfectly legal to broadcast Flynn's name in an intelligence report monitoring a foreign agent.

THE OBAMA FACTOR

Yates's sequence of events doesn't fully jibe with what actually happened. We now know another, more accurate, reason why Flynn wasn't unmasked. It's because he was actively targeted. Or rather, he was discovered in what appears to be a White House–ordered sweep. We know this because Andrew McCabe, the deputy director of the FBI, laid this all out in his self-satisfied book, completely unaware he was revealing the truth about how the Flynn-Kislyak calls were really discovered.

According to McCabe and other ex-Obama administration sources, the White House was stunned by the Russians' reaction to the December Obama-ordered sanctions and the expulsion of the Russian diplomats from both the Maryland and New York Russian compounds. They claim they expected fireworks, but I strongly dispute this. It's more likely that they understood that Putin would wait in favor of gauging the reaction of the soon-to-be Trump administration. Predictably, Putin's peons sat tight and the Russian leader announced that they would not expel anyone in retaliation. Obama's intelligence team feigned shock at this largely predictable move. The president's daily briefing (PDB) team—the group that put together the intelligence overview for Obama every morning—claimed to be especially puzzled. Here's McCabe's version of what happened.

> The PDB staff decided to write an intelligence assessment as to why Putin made the choice that he did. They issued a request to the intelligence community: Anyone who had information on the topic was invited to offer it for consideration. In response to that request, the FBI queried our own holdings. We came across information indicating that General Mike Flynn, the president-elect's nominee for National Security Advisor, had held several conversations with the Russian ambassador to the U.S. Sergey Kislyak in which the sanctions were discussed. This information was something we had since December 29. I had not been aware of it. My impression was that

higher level officials within the FBI counterintelligence division had not been aware of it. The PDB brought it to our attention.

An analyst shared it with me; I shared it with Comey; Comey shared it with the Director of National Intelligence, James Clapper; and Clapper verbally briefed it to President Obama.[16]

Obama's insiders ordered U.S. intelligence and law enforcement to sweep through all recent assets, and the FBI—which had failed to flag the call as suspicious—found exactly what Obama and his team were looking for. The reason there was no unmasking wasn't because it provided context, as Yates suggested. It didn't require an unmasking because the presidential daily briefing staff ordered a probe into Russia's response and the phone call was the answer to that probe. In simpler terms, General Flynn was targeted. His call with Kislyak was hunted down. His call with Kislyak was not monitored as a result of it accidentally falling into some Russian dragnet. Flynn was always the target.

Now remember, Obama already had it in for Flynn. He had fired him previously. In this scenario, Clapper, who also reportedly had a role in dismissing Flynn, came and told the President that Flynn had been doing policy deals on the side. Can you imagine Obama's reaction? He must have been quaking with rage. The mainstream media always portrays Obama as some kind of level-headed saint. But don't you think this would have sent him over the edge? He finally ripped the Russians for their alleged election interference and then found out that Flynn had reached out and spoken to Kislyak. Given all the bad blood Obama and Clapper had for Flynn, does anyone really think the outgoing administration was going to give the general a pass?

Flynn was a dead man walking as soon as the PDB team got the phone call information they needed. And Susan Rice's "by the book" email—written in the last minutes of the exiting administration—seems more and more like an obvious eleventh-hour alibi for Obama and the entire get-Flynn operation.

Of course, there was yet another, unspoken, reason Flynn was identified. To promote a bogus narrative about colluding with Russia and to
destabilize a new administration.

Was this sequence of events chaotic? Likely. Did Flynn's chat with
Kislyak challenge the Obama administration's questionable request to
steer clear of policy discussions with other nations? Yes. But did Flynn's
actions make sense? Absolutely. Trump was going to have to deal with
Russia for the next four years, not Obama. It would have been tacti-
cally and diplomatically asinine for Flynn not to return Kislyak's call.
And it was logical and responsible for the Trump team to want to defuse
tensions with Putin. Flynn was only guilty of doing his job. And come
on, *the guy was on vacation.* For all we know, he might have just had a
well-deserved cocktail or two before he checked his phone and made a
series of calls. Why anyone would expect him to have a perfect recollection of this specific call amid the myriad of things he was dealing with,
given the prominence of his new position, is absurd.

Within a week, however, those calls and conversations were revealed
in intelligence briefings, marking the beginning of the end for Flynn.
But when you look at the tragic chain of events, it's impossible not to
wonder if everything was planned in advance. As soon as the future
national security advisor—a man whom Barack Obama had previously
removed and whom he later bad-mouthed, saying he "wasn't exactly a
fan" of Flynn during a meeting with Trump—flew out of the country,
Obama unleashed sanctions against Russia. It was a huge story and one
that indirectly attacked both Russia and Trump's victory. *Of course*, the
Trump transition team would react. And of course Putin would bristle.
And of course, Flynn would be drawn in.

While he was in the Dominican Republic.

With limited access to secure communications.

There are no coincidences in the cloak-and-dagger world of intelligence gathering. This was a setup.

Part two of a three-act takedown was complete.

THE THIRD SETUP

There was, of course, another reason why Michael Flynn was under a microscope: the FBI investigation into the Trump team, code-named Operation Crossfire Hurricane. Although the FBI team initially opened separate counterintelligence cases on George Papadopoulos, Paul Manafort, and Carter Page on August 10, 2016, one week later they added Flynn to their list. What happened between August 10 and August 16 that convinced the FBI to add Flynn to their list? On August 11, paid spy Stefan Halper met with FBI special agent Stephen Somma, his longtime handler. Do you think Halper might have mentioned the 2014 dinner with Lokhova and Flynn? Someone fitting his description certainly mentioned the dinner to the FBI, as we learned from belated FBI disclosures in the Flynn criminal case. We also know from the IG Report that Halper mentioned Flynn in his meeting.[17] The FBI didn't tip its hand; it simply justified adding the new operation out of concern Flynn "may wittingly or unwittingly be involved in activity on behalf of the Russian Federation which may constitute a federal crime or threat to the national security."[18]

So, it was natural that the Crossfire Hurricane investigators would raise a few eyebrows when, during the FBI's monitoring of Kislyak, they got transcripts of his December 29 call with General Flynn. Given Jim Comey's FBI leadership team's desperate need to stain the incoming administration's reputation, it was also natural that news of the Kislyak call would leak to liberal media activists, thirsty for click-bait, anti-Trump content.

On January 12, 2017, just days before the Trump inauguration, *Washington Post* columnist David Ignatius, citing "a senior U.S. government official," revealed that "Flynn phoned Russian Ambassador Sergey Kislyak several times on Dec. 29, the day the Obama administration announced the expulsion of 35 Russian officials as well as other measures in retaliation for the hacking."[19]

Ignatius buried this information in his article, but it quickly became fuel for anyone in the mainstream media feeding the collusion fantasy. The next day, White House spokesman Sean Spicer denied sanctions were discussed. On January 15, Vice President-elect Mike Pence appeared on *Face the Nation* and said Obama's sanctions weren't mentioned: "They did not discuss anything having to do with the United States' decision to expel diplomats or impose censure against Russia."

Pence was basing his description on what Flynn had told him. But why would Flynn, a trained intelligence professional fully aware of the fact that the FBI likely had verbatim transcripts of the Kislyak call, lie to the vice president of the United States?

I'm not going to answer that question yet, but keep it in the back of your mind.

Pence's TV appearance would prove fatal to Michael Flynn because it *theoretically* put Flynn in a compromising position, according to counter-intelligence experts. Flynn had talked about sanctions with Kislyak. The Russians knew this and therefore—again, theoretically—had leverage over Flynn. They knew he had "lied" to his superior, which might have allowed them to blackmail or otherwise influence an incoming member of Trump's cabinet.

On January 19, Acting Attorney General Sally Yates, Director of National Intelligence James Clapper, CIA Director John Brennan, and FBI Director Jim Comey met to discuss warning Trump that Flynn had misled Spicer and Pence—but Comey, who knew his agents were investigating Flynn for possible collusion, nixed the idea.

The FBI team was plotting to approach Flynn.

Actually, let's call it what it was: they were plotting to set up Flynn.

We know this for a number of reasons.

First and foremost, Jim Comey actually bragged about it on TV. In a December 13, 2018, interview, the former FBI director admitted that his agents arranged an interview with Flynn without asking the White House counsel's office, in violation of established protocols for FBI criminal dealings with the White House. In other words, they actively sought to interview Flynn without a lawyer present—which, by the way, is exactly what the FBI did in their initial interview with George Papadopoulos. That's because lawyers frequently advise their clients not to talk to FBI agents. Comey didn't actually use the word "setup," but he might as well have, saying the Flynn interview was "something I probably wouldn't have done or maybe gotten away with in a more...organized administration."

Comey's use of the phrase "gotten away with" is stunning. He was talking about duping Flynn. Convincing the national security advisor to walk into a legal trap. He and his agents sought to lure Flynn into the easiest trap in all of law enforcement: lying to an FBI agent.

To lull Flynn into a false sense of security, FBI insiders took to the press again, in a leak to the *Washington Post* on January 23 that was clearly designed to put Flynn's mind at ease about this exploding Russia hoax. From the article's headline—"FBI Reviewed Flynn's Calls with Russian Ambassador but Found Nothing Illicit"—to the smaller print, every word of the piece was a classic spin of misdirection, fed to a journalist to create the idea Flynn had nothing to worry about, even though they were about to give him a lot to worry about. "Although Flynn's contacts with Russian Ambassador Sergey Kislyak were listened to, Flynn himself is not the active target of an investigation, U.S. officials said."[20] Yeah, sure.

This report also marked the second time in eleven days that the *Washington Post* ran stories based on leaks involving the FBI and General Flynn. The first, by David Ignatius on January 12, appeared to expose Flynn. The second seemed to give him a pass. Only the journalists who wrote these two stories know for certain who those "U.S. officials" cited are. (According to reports, Ignatius's source may have been Colonel James Baker, the director of the Office of Net Assessment at the Pentagon. The two men reportedly dined together frequently, and Baker, perhaps coincidentally, also approved payments and contracts for key Flynn adversary Stefan Halper.)[21] But it seems pretty clear that those sources were feeding

Ellen Nakashima and Greg Miller of the *Washington Post*, a convincing mix of facts and total misinformation. Flynn, as the IG Report clearly notes, had been a target since, at the latest, August 2016.

Why is this second article part of the setup? Imagine Michael Flynn's mindset at this moment in time. He should be on top of the world. He's got the dream job to protect and defend the United States as the president's national security advisor. He can begin to push for the policies in the Middle East he's always wanted and win the war on terror. He can finally expose the deep-state intelligence failures that have plagued the country's intelligence bureaucracy for decades. But instead, he finds himself in the hot seat himself? He's hearing rumors. He's wondering if he's going to hurt the Trump administration instead of helping it. And then he comes to work and he reads the *Washington Post* article that appears to exonerate him. The article says he's not under investigation. It must have been a great relief considering Flynn knew he had committed no crimes.

And that was exactly what the FBI wanted him to feel. Safe. At ease. Unthreatened. And ready to talk. And that was his mistake. He trusted the FBI, and he viewed them as partners in the fights he was sure to confront ahead in his new national security position. Tragically, this was a big mistake.

On the same day the article appeared, however, Peter Strzok and Lisa Page were feeling very, very nervous. Strzok was gearing up to interview Flynn in the White House the following day. "I can feel my heart beating harder," Lisa Page texted her FBI beau and Flynn tormentor. "I'm so stressed about all the ways THIS has the potential to go fully off the rails."[22]

"I know," Strzok responded.[23]

Flynn was a big deal for Crossfire Hurricane and the top guns at the FBI. There had been a number of deliberations and strategy sessions leading up to the interview. According to the January 4 FBI draft "Closing Communication" memo preparing to end the Flynn probe, the investigation had found no derogatory evidence that Crossfire Razor (Flynn) was compromised by the Russians. The next step was to close the investigation. There was no there, there.

"The absence of any derogatory information or lead information from these logical sources reduce the number of investigative avenues and techniques to pursue. Per the direction of FBI management, Crossfire Razor was not interviewed as part of the case closing procedure. The FBI is closing this investigation" read the memo.[24]

But that same day, Peter Strzok texted his team with a different message: not so fast—FBI senior management on the seventh floor of the FBI headquarters had other ideas about Crossfire Razor, according to a text reported by John Solomon.

"Hey if you haven't closed RAZOR, don't do so yet," Strzok texted on Jan. 4, 2017.

"It is still open and I'm still listed as the case manager" was the response.

"[Roger], I couldn't raise earlier. Please keep it open for now," Strzok texted. In another text, he added where this directive was coming from: "7th floor involved."[25]

The Flynn investigation didn't just remain open; it was heating up, despite previous lack of any evidence. Evidently, the Kislyak phone call represented a new point of attack for Flynn's persistent FBI tormentors. And the investigators grappled with how best to approach Flynn for the setup interview. They had spent four months trying to connect him to the ridiculous Russia collusion fantasy. Now they would get one last chance.

But what did that chance mean? What was the endgame for the investigators at this point? The Manafort investigation was moving along, but most of the charges had to do with money laundering and tax issues entirely unrelated to Russian collusion. The Papadopoulos probe hadn't yielded much either. FBI agents in Chicago had succeeded in interviewing him without a lawyer—and as we now know, they got him on the tried-and-true 1001 charge, the legal code for lying to a federal agent—but Halper and other informants had failed to connect George Papadopoulos to any Russian operation. As for Carter Page, even with all of the surveillance powers of the FISA spying warrant they obtained targeting him, they had found nothing to substantiate the Steele allegations.

Add it all up and they needed to get something on Flynn. Something that might force him to cooperate and spill dirt on others in the Trump orbit.

At the end of April 2020, a slew of FBI records that capture the inner workings of the FBI finally saw the light of day—including the disturbing January 4 information about closing the Flynn probe. They also revealed that at least one supervisory member of the Crossfire Hurricane team, FBI senior manager Bill Priestap according to multiple reports, had major reservations about going after Flynn. A handwritten note dated January 24, 2017 (although the "4" in "24" appears in much darker ink, possibly suggesting it may have been altered), bearing the initials EP (Edward William Priestap is the full name of the assistant director of the FBI Counterintelligence Division), was filled with tactical and ethical questions about the Flynn inquiry.

The notes reveal that Priestap had second thoughts about gunning for Flynn. I "agreed yesterday that we shouldn't show Flynn [REDACTED] if he didn't admit," Priestap wrote. "I thought [about] it last night, [and] I believe we should rethink this."[26]

Then he asked the big question that the entire document grapples with: "What's our goal? Truth/admission or to get him to lie, so we can prosecute him or get him fired?"

Elsewhere on the page, he provided an answer: "We have a case on Flynn and Russians," he wrote, adding "our goal is to resolve [the] case. Our goal is to determine if Mike Flynn is going to tell the truth [about] his relationship [with] Russians."

Priestap then focused on tactics and the endgame. He seemed to be weighing working cooperatively with Flynn, rather than antagonistically.

"We regularly show subjects evidence, with the goal of getting them to admit wrongdoing," he wrote. "I don't see how getting someone to admit their wrongdoing is going easy on him."

He also indicated that working to charge Flynn with a Logan Act violation is something best left to the Department of Justice: "Give the facts to the DoJ, and let them decide."

But the most damning part in the entire document shows Priestap was wary of the Crossfire Hurricane team setting up Flynn to fail with an unnecessary interview, about a call with Kislyak they already had the transcript of, and about Russian collusion allegations regarding Flynn that they had *already debunked.* It comes at the very end in the document as a brief, two-sentence prophetic warning:

"If we're seen as playing games, [the White House] will be furious," the author wrote. "Protect our institution by not playing games." Sounds like Priestap was covering his own ass for the outcry he knew was coming when this asinine scheme was uncovered.

Those games included discussions about whether Strzok would have an obligation to inform Flynn that lying to FBI agents was a crime. Emails between Lisa Page and Strzok sought to clarify this issue, as well as debate whether Flynn should be told this at the beginning of the interview or after he might say something the FBI knew was untrue? Why scheme to downplay the significance of a lie to a federal agent; maybe because they were hoping for a misstep and wanted Flynn's guard down? Emphasizing the consequences would have done the opposite.

One day after the January 4, 2017, back-and-forth about closing and not closing the Flynn probe, FBI Director James Comey met with President Obama, Vice President Joe Biden, Acting Attorney General Sally Yates, and others. This Spygate brain trust discussed whether the FBI and others in the intel community thought conversations with the Trump transition team about Russia should be limited because of concerns members of the incoming president's team might be compromised, according to multiple reports. We also know this happened because it

was the same January 5 meeting covered in the "Obama's Fixer" chapter
that Susan Rice documented by writing a bizarre email to herself memorializing the conversation. That's the letter where she reported Obama
"reiterated our law enforcement team needs to proceed as it normally
would by the book."

What is not in Rice's letter is what happened at the end of the meeting. An FBI 302 memo summarizing an interview with Sally Yates reveals
the acting attorney general first learned about the Flynn-Kislyak phone
calls *from President Obama*.

Here is the relevant passage:

> Obama dismissed the group but asked Yates and Comey to stay
> behind. Obama started by saying he had "learned of the information
> about Flynn" and his conversation with Kislyak about sanctions.
> Obama specified he did not want any additional information on the
> matter, but was seeking information on whether the White House
> should be treating Flynn any differently, given the information. At
> that point, Yates had no idea what the President was talking about,
> but figured it out based on the conversation. Yates recalled Comey
> mentioning the Logan Act, but can't recall if he specified there was
> an "investigation"…It was not clear to Yates from where the Pres-
> ident first received the information. Yates did not recall Comey's
> response to the President's question about how to treat Flynn. She
> was so surprised by the information she was hearing that she was
> having a hard time processing it and listening to the conversation
> at the same time."[27]

Where did Obama learn about the calls? It may have been included
in the President's Daily Brief, the summary of high-level national security
issues written up with input from cabinet members and the intelligence
community. Or it may have been another one of John Brennan's "non-of-
ficial" channels briefs to President Obama. While it is curious Yates didn't
make this assumption, the more interesting thing about this exchange is
that Obama had zeroed in on Flynn and immediately wanted to discuss

it with his top legal and investigative officers. Once again Flynn was on the president's radar and he was now putting Flynn on Yates and Comey's radar too. While Yates said Obama couched his concern in "how the White House should be treating" Flynn, you have to wonder what Comey's take-away was from the president's Flynn-focus. Did he interpret this as an invitation to pursue Flynn further with the president's blessing? While that is possible, since just one day earlier FBI leadership had made sure the Flynn probe hadn't been closed, it seems more likely that Comey was already all in on Flynn.

The FBI's Yates interview also provides a window into Comey's involvement in the January 25 interview setup of Flynn. Comey called Yates to say that two agents—Peter Strzok and Joe Pientka—were on their way to interview Flynn. Yates's description of the call can be read as Comey having a J. Edgar Hoover moment of going all maverick. "Yates was very frustrated in the call with Comey. She felt a decision to conduct an interview of Flynn should have been coordinated with the DOJ. There were trial attorneys at [the National Security Division] working with the FBI and it was not 'solely' an investigation. In Yates' view, the prosecutors should be involved in coordinating the type of approach and interview questions. She also thought there should have been a discussion about recording the interview. In raising these things with Comey, he said something like 'you can understand why I did this,' to which Yates replied 'no' and Comey responded he didn't want it to 'look political.' Yates was offended by the implication."[28]

On January 6, the intel quartet of Comey, Clapper, Brennan, and Rogers briefed Trump, as I related in my chapter on Brennan. The purpose of the meeting was twofold. Officially, the plan was to brief Trump on the findings of the Intelligence Community Assessment, which was released that same day. The assessment focused on Russian election interference and questionably concluded "with high confidence that…Putin ordered an influence campaign in 2016 aimed at the US presidential election."

The Russian campaign goals were to undermine faith in the election process and deny Hillary Clinton the presidency.[29]

After the presentation of the assessment to Trump and his National Security Team, the plan was for Clapper, Brennan, Rogers, and Trump's team to leave so that Comey could have a private discussion with Trump. And that is exactly what happened. Comey informed the president-elect of the ridiculous, putrid allegations made in the Steele dossier involving salacious recordings involving Trump and prostitutes, which I don't even want to dignify by furnishing more details. By discussing these allegations, Comey and company pulled a fast one. Word leaked that the Steele dossier had been discussed with the president-elect, which gave the mainstream media an excuse to now report on Steele's garbage and provided "justification" for Buzzfeed to publish the entire—and entirely dubious—document.

All this went down perfectly for the takedown trio of Comey, Clapper, and Brennan (then-NSA head Rogers was more circumspect in his analysis of the Intelligence Community Assessment's conclusions about Russia's intentions). But we know that there was one uncomfortable and critical hiccup. It was buried in the middle of the IG's massive report, and it hints that Mike Flynn was onto the FBI's use of unreliable sources. Here is the key passage:

> According to an email Comey sent to FBI officials on January 7, 2017, Comey mentioned during the initial portion of the briefing a piece of Steele's reporting that indicated Russia had files of derogatory information on both Clinton and the President-elect. Comey's email stated that a member of Trump's national security team asked during the briefing whether the FBI was "trying to dig into the subsources" to gain a better understanding of the situation, and Comey responded in the affirmative.[30]

Who was the "member of Trump's national security team"? I've been told by informed sources it was none other than Flynn. This makes perfect sense. Flynn was Trump's national security advisor, so of course he was there. Plus, he was intimately familiar with intelligence gathering and the FBI's use of "subsources."

By asking this question, though, Flynn likely made himself a bigger target than he already was. This exchange was filled with unspoken implications. Flynn was making it clear he knew that the reports Comey mentioned concerning derogatory information were suspect and needed to be fully vetted. Meanwhile, Comey must have realized that Trump's soon-to-be right-hand man was on to the FBI's politicized intel laundering operation. Flynn wasn't in charge yet, but he was already pushing Comey to probe his operatives and verify the information they were providing. What was going to happen when Flynn became the national security advisor and pushed Trump to dig deeper? It was Comey's worst nightmare; he realized Flynn was gearing up to take down the bogus Russiagate investigation. The general was about to call Comey's elaborate Steele-reinforced bluff.

To prevent that, Comey needed to take down Flynn first. It was a race against time for the FBI director.

How did Flynn know the FBI subsources were so suspect? There's reason to believe he was tipped off by the British government. Flynn's lawyer Sidney Powell says a letter was "delivered by the British Embassy to the incoming National Security team after Donald Trump's election, and to outgoing National Security Adviser Susan Rice." According to Powell, who was asking for the letter to be released by the FBI, the communication "apparently disavows former British Secret Service Agent Christopher Steele, calls his credibility into question and declares him untrustworthy."[31] It is not clear exactly when this missive was sent, but the Intelligence Assessment meeting was nearly two months after Trump's election win—plenty of time for diplomatic channels to send an appraisal of the increasingly circulated dossier.

This letter has not surfaced, as far as we know. But how did Powell learn about it? Flynn must have seen it. This seems likely because as soon as Comey mentioned some aspect of Steele's Russian collusion fantasy,

Flynn began questioning Comey. The fact that this letter hasn't surfaced is not surprising. As the deluge of shocking documents finally released in April 2020 shows, Brandon Van Grack, a Justice Department prosecutor and former member of Special Counsel Robert Mueller's team, seems to have repeatedly failed to produce favorable evidence to Flynn, as required by Judge Emmet Sullivan's February 16, 2018, court order. That declaration directed "the government to produce…any evidence in its possession that is favorable to defendant and material either to defendant's guilt or punishment" in a timely manner.[32] Unfortunately, Van Grack had trouble complying, judging by the flood of exculpatory evidence that finally surfaced in 2020 thanks in part to the DOJ-ordered investigations into the origins of the Russia investigation and the Flynn probe.

On January 24, it was time to initiate the key step in the takedown plan. Remember that interview where Comey admitted to the interview ambush? The one in which he bragged, "I sent them," and admitted the FBI bypassed typical interview protocol in order to blindside Flynn? "I thought: 'It's early enough, let's just send a couple of guys over,'" he recounted.[33]

Actually, it seems that Comey's deputy director Andrew McCabe did the initial heavy lifting. At 12:30 he picked up the phone and called Flynn and arranged a meeting for 2:30 that afternoon, telling Flynn the FBI needed to talk to him in light of the "media coverage and public discussion about his recent contacts with Russian representatives."

The two guys sent over were Peter Strzok and Joe Pientka, the man identified in the inspector general's report as Supervisory Special Agent 1 of the Crossfire Hurricane investigation (Pientka is knee-deep in this scandal and was also the agent responsible for maintaining the "Woods File" for Crossfire Hurricane, the file where the FBI failed to verify the allegations in Steele's dossier). Strzok asked the questions and Pientka took notes. Those notes were then collated and written up by Strzok in a 302, the FBI's official form to summarize an interview. According to the 302, Strzok asked Flynn several questions about his interactions with Russian ambassador Kislyak. At one point, Flynn explained that he "has no particular affinity for Russia, but that Kislyak was his counterpart, and maintaining trusted relationships with foreign governments is important."[34]

The interview touched on several other Russia-related issues and a series of calls he made to foreign governments about a UN resolution regarding Israeli settlements. Then Strzok got down to business. He asked Flynn if he recalled a conversation with Kislyak "surrounding the expulsion of Russian diplomats or the closing of Russian properties in response to Russian hacking activities surrounding the election." Flynn said the conversation was about something else and noted he didn't have access to his government Blackberry or TV news. Strzok then asked if he remembered if he might have asked Kislyak to refrain from escalating the situation or engage in a "tit-for-tat."[35]

"Not really. I don't remember. It wasn't 'don't do anything.'"

Asked about a follow-up call with Kislyak, where the ambassador allegedly stated Russia had chosen to moderate its response as a result of the incoming administration's request, Flynn "stated it was possible he had talked to Kislyak on the issue, but if he did, he did not remember doing so." Flynn also said he remembered making a number of phone calls to Kislyak because he experienced connectivity problems.[36]

Summarizing this exchange in a court document, Robert Mueller wrote: "During the interview, the FBI agents gave the defendant multiple opportunities to correct his false statements by revisiting key questions. When the defendant said he did not remember something they knew he said, they used the exact words the defendant had used in order to prompt a truthful response. But the defendant never corrected his false statements."

Okay. By now, everyone gets it. The FBI alleges Flynn lied. But here's the thing: Mike Flynn is an intelligence expert. He must have known Kislyak's phone was monitored. He had read the *Washington Post* story that suggested the call was tracked. And then he told Sean

Spicer and Mike Pence that he hadn't discussed Russia's response to sanctions. Then he told Peter Strzok he didn't remember. The general was remarkably consistent.

Months after meeting Flynn, Peter Strzok was quizzed about the talk. This interview of the FBI veteran was written up as a 302 and suspiciously filed months later on August 22, 2017. The document reports that Strzok described the interview subject this way:

> Flynn had a very "sure" demeanor and did not give any indicators of deception. He did not parse his words or hesitate in any of his answers…. Strzok and Pientka both had the impression at the time that Flynn was not lying or did not think he was lying."[37]

This is puzzling. An intelligence veteran on at least three different occasions told people that he did not have a specific conversation. Or that he didn't remember the details in the same way it was reported by U.S. intelligence sources. If the veteran knew that lying to FBI agents was a crime—and presumably he did—and he believed the FBI had evidence of that call or calls, why on earth would he deny the call or say he didn't remember? To get back to a question I posed earlier, why would Michael Flynn lie to the vice president?

Is it possible that Flynn forgot about the call? Or the details of the call? Seriously. The man was on vacation. Did he make the call and then go out and join the conga line with his wife? Did he party a little bit? Or, hell, did he party up a storm? I have no idea. I'm just saying none of his alleged behavior makes sense unless he honestly, completely forgot some of the details of the call. Something every one of us does every day when trying to recall details of our interactions.

One of the great mysteries of the Flynn investigation swirls around the actual records of those Flynn calls. The FBI guarded the transcripts like they were sacred treasure. And Department of Justice prosecutors even rebuffed a federal judge's attempt to obtain the transcripts. In May 2019, Judge Emmet Sullivan, the judge overseeing Flynn's sentencing, ordered the Mueller team to provide a transcript of the Flynn-Kislyak call. It was a surprising move. In a previous hearing, Sullivan made it clear that all the FBI's work, all the hearsay evidence, leaks, innuendo, and spin had done their damage; the judge was convinced of Flynn's guilt. When Flynn balked over setting a date for sentencing, Sullivan wasn't happy. Flynn had a legitimate beef. He was upset that the prosecution, which had previously stated Flynn's "substantial assistance" to the government merited leniency, recommended a sentence of between zero to six months in prison.

Sullivan ripped into the general, at one point even suggesting Flynn's behavior was treasonous.

"This is a very serious offense," he said. "A high-ranking senior official of the government making false statements to the Federal Bureau of Investigation while on the physical premises of the White House."

Then he referenced other alleged accusations that had leaked into the press. "All along, you were an unregistered agent of a foreign country while serving as the national security adviser to the president of the United States," he said. "Arguably, that undermines everything this flag over here stands for. Arguably, you sold your country out." The blistering bias continued with this remark: "I'm not hiding my disgust, my disdain, for this criminal offense."

Although Sullivan walked back his "selling the country out" statement, it was clear that, just like Obama, he was no fan of Flynn, so the request to see the transcript—the actual proof that Flynn said what the FBI said he said—was a bit of a surprise.

Unfortunately, one month later, Mueller's legal snakes wriggled their way out of providing it—insisting it was never part of the evidentiary record. Here's the key line, which comes after the prosecutors revealed Flynn provided a copy of a voicemail message from Trump's lawyer John Dowd to Flynn's lawyer Rob Kelner on the eve of Flynn's plea deal: "The government further represents it is not relying on any other recordings, of any person, for the purposes of establishing the defendant's guilt or determining his sentencing, nor are there any other recordings that are part of the sentencing record." Sullivan later agreed the transcript did not need to be provided.

For nearly four years, no official transcript of the call that had landed Flynn in so much trouble saw the light of day.

You could be excused for wondering why the prosecutors were bending over backwards to keep it under wraps.

We'll get to the answer soon.

THE SLEEPER ACTIVATION

Tape or no tape, Flynn was destroyed by the interview with Strzok. But Acting Attorney General, and Spygate player, Sally Yates detonated Flynn's expulsion from the White House. On January 26, two days after Strzok's interview with Flynn, she set up a meeting with White House Counsel Don McGahn. She walked McGahn through Flynn's alleged misdeeds—asserting that Flynn had misled Pence. In her line of reasoning, as she later testified, she was concerned the Russians "likely had proof." If that was true, it "created a compromise situation, a situation where the national security adviser essentially could be blackmailed by the Russians."

Nearly two weeks after the McGahn conversation, the content of the calls between Flynn and Kislyak were leaked to the *Washington Post*, which ran the story on February 9. The *New York Times* quickly followed with a more alarmist piece, asserting the calls were "unambiguous and highly inappropriate," according to officials.

The storyline that Flynn had misled Pence went viral.

Flynn was now damaged goods at the White House. He resigned on February 13, less than four weeks after he was appointed national security advisor. The phone call setup executed in the Dominican Republic had done the damage and destroyed a decorated member of our military and a genuine American hero.

Meanwhile, Peter Strzok's interview made the already wounded Flynn vulnerable to prosecution. According to the FBI, he had committed a felony by lying to two FBI agents. That setup—an interview without lawyers present—worked, too. He pled guilty on December 1, 2017.

On February 19, 2017, six days after Flynn had been forced to resign over the Kislyak phone calls, the Cambridge dinner operation Stefan Halper had worked on, was activated. It began with a nasty, innuendo-filled piece by a guest at the 2014 dinner, Christopher Andrew, in the *Sunday Times*. Andrew cited Flynn's "evident pleasure in engaging with some of the seminar's talented postgraduates." Flynn, he wrote, "was especially struck by one bilingual postgraduate, with dual British-Russian nationality," who showed him an erotic postcard sent by Stalin.

Andrew never named the postgraduate, to be clear. But he was alluding to Lokhova, with whom he worked.

According to Andrew, Flynn invited this woman to work as a translator on his next official visit to Moscow. Andrew then claimed that although that trip was canceled, "Flynn continued an —unclassified— email correspondence with her on Russian history, occasionally signing himself 'General Misha'—Russian for 'Mike.'"

A candidate for the author of the most disingenuous newspaper article in history, Andrew claimed he was sharing this anecdote to demonstrate Flynn's maverick qualities—"striking evidence of his spontaneity and impatience with bureaucratic routine" and "his instinct when he sees a new opportunity is to follow it up." For anyone capable of reading between the lines, he was floating a much different story—that Flynn may have fallen for a classic honeypot intelligence sting.

Why activate this tale from 2014 in 2017, after Flynn had been fired by Trump?

The answers should be pretty obvious. The FBI was piling on. This was yet another angle to savage Flynn's reputation and to taint the Trump administration with more specters of Russian collaboration. It put more pressure on Flynn to cut a deal with prosecutors. Although the special counsel had yet to be appointed, it seems clear, once the FBI thought they had a case against Flynn—even a desperate 1001 "lying to a Federal Agent" charge—they would use it.

The details of Halper's operation and his coordination with mainstream media can be found in the publications of four of Halper's co-defendants named in Lokhova's suit, who are all in the news business (Dow Jones publishes the *Wall Street Journal*). From that single brief encounter between Flynn and Lokhova, Halper managed to spin an elaborate campaign, according to both Lokhova's lawsuit and the public record. Here's her take: "Halper colluded with operatives at Cambridge University, and agents employed by Dow Jones, the Guardian, the *Times* and the Post to leak false statements about [Lokhova] as part of a nefarious effort to smear General Flynn and fuel and further the now debunked and dead narrative that the Trump campaign colluded with Russia."

Boom!

Lokhova's lawsuit also refuted almost all of Andrew's article. She charged that Andrew instigated the meeting between her and Flynn and that Andrew asked her to stay in contact with Flynn because he hoped General Flynn might work with the seminar or the institute. Lokhova occasionally emailed Flynn, according to her filing, which stated Andrew "saw all the email exchanges, which were general in nature. At no point did General Flynn sign any emails as 'General Misha'. General Flynn never invited Lokhova to Moscow on an official visit or otherwise."[38]

The entire innuendo-filled story was nothing more than a media hit—one that Halper's buddies delivered, and that Halper then promoted, according to the suit. Among the Lokhova lawsuit's other charges: Halper told *Wall Street Journal* reporters that she and Flynn had an affair, and made similar calls to the *Daily Mail* and the *Telegraph* in which he disparaged her and Flynn.

But perhaps the most explosive revelation in the entire suit is that Halper—who we now know was an FBI informant and associate as well as a contractor for the Department of Defense—gave an interview on

BBC radio in which he basically referenced the Deep State that kept him so busy.

"People are deeply concerned about the erratic nature of this White House," Halper said on the air, targeting Trump. He added there was "frustration that the country is lacking a coherent and focused leadership" and a "broad sense that this president may not have the proper skills for this job."

Who were these "people"? Halper's bosses? Was it Comey, McCabe, Strzok, and Somma? Was it Clapper and Brennan and Yates? Were they "exhibiting coherent and focused leadership"—by ordering and abetting sting operations on members of Trump's administration? Halper appears to have been the shining example of an informant running amok, in an agency that was out to remove a president. What else could he be alluding to when he suggested the president doesn't have the skills for the job?

Ultimately, the evidence suggests Stefan Halper wasn't just out to destroy Mike Flynn—although he appears to have given it his best try—he was out to destroy Trump.

As for Lieutenant General Michael Flynn, the proud army veteran with thirty years of service, whom the FBI painted as a treasonous spy instead of a patriot who sought to depoliticize American intelligence operations and focus on shutting down anti-American jihadists forever?

He was just the wreckage created by Operation Crossfire Hurricane spinning out of control.

Yes, he was a target. But like so many others caught in the FBI and Mueller team's desperate scramble to destabilize and remove Trump, he was—in their eyes—nothing more than collateral damage.

THE SCALES OF JUSTICE RECALIBRATE

When I started writing this chapter, it never occurred to me that Michael Flynn's story could or would have a happy ending. When America's most powerful law enforcement entity pours resources into fabricating a case against you, what chance do you have?

But, amazingly, Mike Flynn and his tenacious lawyer Sidney Powell caught a break.

In early 2020, Attorney General William Barr appointed Jeff Jensen, a prosecutor out of the U.S. Attorney's Office in St. Louis, to reexamine the handling of the Flynn case. He and other attorneys interviewed DOJ prosecutors involved in the case, revisited documents, and located previously unseen ones. Among those that surfaced and were shared with Flynn's defense team were many of the papers I've already cited, including FBI 302s, Bill Priestap's notes as he wrestled with the goals of the case, and the FBI draft document closing the Flynn probe—which, ironically, had been approved by Agent Joe Pientka, the agent who accompanied Peter Strzok to interview Flynn. These documents underscored the tenuousness of the case against Flynn and helped firm up a timeline for the FBI probe, establishing when agents made decisions and what they were based on. They also helped establish the clear setup of the White House interview to take Flynn down by inducing him to lie to FBI agents.

Informed by these documents and the FBI's undue focus on Flynn, Jensen also revisited the wording of the charge and its intent. Jensen's reasoning might best be summed up this way by taking these facts into account:

- The Crossfire Hurricane investigation that brought Flynn to the FBI's attention was specifically about the possible coordination with Russia to interfere with the 2016 election.
- The FBI had found no wrongdoing, or any "derogatory information," on Flynn's part with regard to any Russian coordination or election interference.
- The interview that Strzok and Pientka conducted—in which Flynn allegedly lied, resulting in the charge against him—had nothing to do with the election.
- Flynn was denied access to the papers that established he had been exonerated prior to the interview.[39]

Add all that up, and Jensen and others at the Department of Justice realized, as the government eventually stated in its dismissal motion, the case against Flynn had focused on "continued prosecution of false statements that were not 'material' to any bona fide investigation."

In other words, even if Flynn had lied or innocently misremembered, it didn't matter. The interview had nothing to do with any credible investigation.

"Through the course of my review of General Flynn's case, I concluded the proper and just course was to dismiss the case," Jensen said in a statement. "I briefed Attorney General Barr on my findings, advised him on these conclusions, and he agreed."[40]

On May 7, 2020, the DOJ submitted a proposed order for Judge Emmet Sullivan to dismiss the case with prejudice. It was uncertain whether Sullivan would accept the prosecutor's recommendation. In fact, it seemed likely that he would order more hearings before making his final ruling. Then, on June 24, 2020, the D.C. Circuit Court of Appeals ordered Sullivan to accept the Justice Department's motion to dismiss the case against Flynn. As this book was going to press, it was unclear if Sullivan would contest the order by requesting an en banc hearing with the full Appeals court or possibly ask the Supreme Court to hear the case.[41]

If Judge Sullivan does ever hold a trial, he will also have one more piece of evidence to weigh: the actual transcript of the call that Flynn supposedly lied about. This is the transcript that the prosecutors refused to produce, claiming it was immaterial to the case. That was a stupefyingly disingenuous argument. If the call wasn't important, then why was lying about the call important? Amazingly, Sullivan seemed to buy the prosecutor's argument. But the transcript was finally released at the end of May 2020 by National Intelligence Director John Ratcliffe, and Judge Sullivan is going to have to reconcile some glaring discrepancies between what Flynn was charged with by Robert Mueller's prosecution team and what he discussed with Peter Strzok. Looking over the transcript and the charging document, it almost seems like the indictment is the fourth setup of Mike Flynn.

DECRYPTING THE TRANSCRIPT

The charging document that Mike Flynn pleaded guilty to asserts that during a January 24, 2017, interview with FBI agents, Flynn "falsely stated that he did not ask Russia's Ambassador to the United States ('Russian Ambassador') to refrain from escalating the situation in response to sanctions that the United States had imposed against Russia. FLYNN also falsely stated that he did not remember a follow-up conversation in which the Russian Ambassador stated that Russia had chosen to moderate its response to those sanctions as a result of FLYNN's request."[42]

The papers then outline a sequence of events: Obama announcing "sanctions against Russia in response to that government's actions intended to interfere with the 2016 presidential election ('U.S. Sanctions')"; Flynn calling Russian Ambassador Kislyak and requesting "that Russia not escalate the situation and only respond to the U.S. Sanctions in a reciprocal manner"; Putin's December 30, 2016, "statement indicating that Russia would not take retaliatory measures in response to the U.S. Sanctions at that time"; and Kislyak's December 31, 2016, call to Flynn that confirmed Russia had chosen not to retaliate thanks to Flynn's request.

The vast majority of the language in the document relates to "U.S. sanctions." But Obama announced "a number of actions" against Russia on December 29. Here's his description of Executive Order 13757:

"I have sanctioned nine entities and individuals: the GRU and the FSB, two Russian intelligence services; four individual officers of the GRU; and three companies that provided material support to the GRU's cyber operations."

Separate from the sanctions or "U.S. Sanctions," per the charging document, were the expulsion of Russian officials and the closure of two Russian properties allegedly used to gather intelligence. Here's more from Obama: "The State Department is also shutting down two Russian compounds, in Maryland and New York, used by Russian personnel for intelligence-related purposes, and is declaring 'persona non grata' 35 Russian intelligence operatives."

So, the sanctions were clearly different from the expulsions. But Flynn only specifically referred to the expulsions on the Kislyak call:

> **Depending on what uh, actions they take over this current issue of the cyber stuff, you know, where they're looking like they're gonna, they're gonna dismiss some number of Russians out of the country... what I would ask Russia to do is to not - is - is - if anything - because I know you have to have some sort of action - to, to only make it reciprocal. Make it reciprocal. Don't – don't make it – don't go any further than you have to. Because I don't want us to get into something that has to escalate, on a, you know, on a tit for tat. You follow me, Ambassador?**

Later in the conversation, he returned to the expulsions issue. His focus remained on not embarking on a series of escalations. "If you have to do something, do something on a reciprocal basis, meaning you know, on a sort of an even basis. Then that, then that is a good message and we'll understand that message," he said before describing a worst-case scenario where the U.S. bounced "30 guys and you send out 60, you know, or you shut down every Embassy."

At no point did he initiate discussions about the sanctions.

In other words, Mike Flynn never mentioned the specific thing he was accused of lying about to the FBI—sanctions!

Ambassador Kislyak was the only one who uttered the S-word, and when he did, he was not even talking about how Russia would respond. He was talking about the implications of fighting terrorism. "One of the problems among the measures that have been announced today is that now FSB and GRU are sanctions, are *sanctioned, and I ask myself, uh— does it mean that the United States isn't willing to work on terrorist threats?"*

And what did Flynn say in response? "Yeah, yeah."

And that was the entire exchange about "sanctions."

Why is this so important? Because the charging document says Flynn lied about discussing sanctions with the FBI, but the FBI 302 written by Peter Strzok doesn't ask Flynn about sanctions.

> The interviewing agents asked FLYNN if he recalled any conversation with KISLYAK in which expulsions were discussed where FLYNN might have encouraged KISLYAK not to escalate the situation, to keep the Russian response reciprocal, or not to engage in a "tit-for-tat." FLYNN responded, "Not really. I don't remember. It wasn't 'Don't do anything.'"[43]

That, if anything, is Flynn's big lie. That he didn't remember.

Can you say witch hunt?

But let's not get sidetracked. Flynn was charged with lying about sanctions. But Strzok didn't ask him about sanctions. In other words, the prosecutor who led this prosecutorial farce, Brandon Van Grack, screwed up big time when he wrote out the charging document. Evidently, he thought the expulsions could be grouped as part of the sanctions. But they are two different things. Two very different things, as Obama made clear in his statement announcing his "Response to Russian Malicious Cyber Activity and Harassment."

Stephen McIntyre, a Canadian climate change expert with a strong interest in conservative politics, has conducted some forensic studies on the Flynn documents and notes that by December 4, 2018, Van Grack realized the definition of U.S. sanctions in the indictment failed to cover the questions and answers in Strzok's 302 on the interview. In a sentencing memorandum written on December 18, 2018, Van Grack broadened the language around the charge, adding "other measures against Russia" into his definition of sanctions. Here's his smooth move:

> Days prior to the FBI's interview of the defendant, the *Washington Post* had published a story alleging that he had spoken with Russia's ambassador to the United States on December 29, 2016, the day

the United States announced sanctions and other measures against Russia in response to that government's actions intended to interfere with the 2016 election (collectively, "sanctions").[44]

This is likely why Van Grack and others worked so hard to prevent the transcript of the Flynn-Kislyak conversation from being entered as evidence! The document would prove that Flynn never mentioned sanctions.

And if he never mentioned them, he hadn't lied to the FBI about not discussing them.

Will Judge Sullivan recognize the prosecutor's botched wording and the nuanced issue of Van Grack's poorly worded and therefore incorrect indictment? I sincerely hope so. The transcripts, as a whole, show Flynn did nothing wrong.

Or will the judge buy into the idea that since Kislyak mentioned "sanctions," Flynn had in fact participated in a discussion about Obama's penalties?

After all the evidence I've laid out here, it seems obvious that the FBI and Mueller's team were obsessed with getting Mike Flynn and that Sullivan should do the right and just thing. If he does, then Lieutenant General Michael Flynn's nightmare may finally be over.

It is unclear what the future holds for the FBI agents, leaders, and confidential human sources who unleashed the legal assault against him.

CHAPTER 8

Whistleblowing in the Dark

I began this book by touching on the impeachment fiasco that arose out of a business-as-usual phone call between President Trump and Ukraine's President Zelensky on July 25, 2019. Revisiting the farce that ensued from this call should be painful to anyone who cares about America, decency, and the rule of law. Those who bought into the claim that President Trump was engaged in, rather than exposing, wrongdoing on the call are living in a fantasy land.

The word diplomacy has come to suggest tactful, polite negotiation to most people. But politicians, leaders, and diplomats all try to exert influence, and they use a wide array of tools to achieve their goals. Diplomacy isn't always "diplomatic," as strange as that may sound. One of the best lines about diplomacy I've ever read was from Henry Wotton, an English ambassador to Venice in the seventeenth century. He said, "An ambassador is an honest man sent to lie abroad for the good of his country."[1]

It's a funny line. And cynical. But largely true.

And as it relates to the Ukraine phone call, it is probably too cynical. There were no lies told during the call. The conversation between Trump and Zelensky was about aid. It was also about two leaders building an alliance for the future. Did President Trump mention "Biden's son"? He did. Did he prevent Ukraine from receiving the $391 million aid package awarded by Congress?[2] No, he did not. Ukraine received the aid in question. Case closed, right? Wrong. Because the Democrats can't take "no" for an answer when it comes to Trump. And if there's no evidence of a controversy, then they'll just fabricate it.

If anything, the cynicism came afterwards, when Democrats cried that the sky was falling because President Trump asked another foreign leader to look into a controversial, politically fraught issue. An issue smacking of the vice president's son's influence-peddling to enrich himself, and which featured the vice president publicly bragging that he had meddled in the law enforcement activities of a foreign country.

Administration critics will rant about Trump's intent during the call, but that is nothing more than speculation masked as fact-finding. These cynics will pontificate about the inferences that can be extracted from the exchange. Again, that's nothing more than interpretation. And they will moan about the supposed optics of Trump's request, which is odd considering that no interpretation is necessary regarding Joe Biden's video-recorded statements where he stated that he had demanded the firing of a Ukrainian prosecutor—a prosecutor who intended to investigate Burisma, the Ukrainian firm that had placed Biden's son on its board—in order to obtain a $1 billion loan.

In the end, however, nothing untoward happened on the Trump-Zelensky call.

How could there be a quid pro quo when the supposed "demand" was never executed? If anything, there was a tit-for-*no*-tat. Ukraine got the military aid it needed, and it did not initiate a much-needed investigation into Burisma and the Bidens.

If you watched this Schiff-show, you might feel that every tiny detail was trotted out in the endless hearings. Who said what? When did they say it? Who else heard it, and what did they think it meant? It was like a political version of Abbott and Costello's famous "Who's on First?" routine.

But what the nation witnessed was selective granularity and storytelling in the form of liberal and biased-media fairy tales. Adam Schiff, who led the Trump-Ukraine impeachment inquiry as the chair of the House Intelligence Committee and was appointed the lead impeachment manager in the subsequent hearing in the Senate, painted a story of a giant conspiracy and a cover-up. But the president released the transcript of the call because he was confident of his own words and intent during the call. Where was the cover-up in that? If this was a cover-up, it was assuredly the worst "cover-up" in American history.

Ironically, Schiff and his anti-Trump allies throughout the government had their own secrets hidden from the nation. A CIA staffer has been publicly and repeatedly identified as the (once-anonymous) whistleblower who set the entire scandal in motion. If he has been correctly identified, then there is a long and disturbing trail that ties him to Schiff and others. These connections, in fact, built up steam as the Democrats moved in, armed with bizarre legal arguments, for their last chance at removing Trump.

THE MOLE

Initially, the only information that surfaced about the anonymous whistleblower was that it was a CIA analyst who had been detailed to the White House and then reassigned to agency headquarters in Langley. On October 30, 2019, RealClearInvestigations reported that that description matched a government official named Eric Ciaramella and that his name had been mentioned in impeachment depositions. The article made a compelling argument for unmasking the alleged whistleblower, who detonated a slow-motion firestorm by filing a complaint with Intelligence Community Inspector General Michael Atkinson on August 12, 2019. That same day, the alleged whistleblower also sent a letter to intelligence chairs Richard Burr and Adam Schiff that was an unclassified summary of his complaint. In it, the author claimed he had "received information from multiple government officials that the President of the United States is using the power of his office to solicit interference from a foreign country in the 2020 U.S. election."[3]

RealClearInvestigations justified identifying Ciaramella as the suspected whistleblower by citing a concern raised by Inspector General Atkinson, who "identified some indicia of an arguable political bias on the part of the Complainant in favor of a rival political candidate."[4] If the complaint about a phone call—which the whistleblower did not actually hear—was driven by bias, his or her identity was an absolutely legitimate part of the story.[5]

Since that article appeared, other outlets followed suit, asserting that Eric Ciaramella was "the alleged whistleblower." As we have seen in the targeting of General Michael Flynn, the reporting on the Trump Tower meeting, and so many other Russiagate angles, the press is far from infallible and, in many cases, they've been part of the disinformation. But in this case, the evidence suggests that concerns about the whistleblower being biased are justified.

Ciaramella, thirty-three years old at the time he was named as the alleged whistleblower, was a registered Democrat. He first arrived at the White House during the Obama administration, working as Ukraine director on the National Security Council, a position later filled by Lieutenant Colonel Alexander Vindman. During the start of the Trump administration, Ciaramella was acting senior director for European and Russian affairs until he was replaced by Fiona Hill. So, like Anthony Ferrante, the FBI's cybersecurity insider in the White House, Ciaramella was a holdover from the previous regime.

Ciaramella, a multilingual Ivy league graduate, had also worked with former Vice President Joe Biden and former CIA Director John Brennan, according to RealClear's Paul Sperry. It's hardly a surprise that Ciaramella, a CIA staffer, should have a connection to the head of the agency.

But it is a red flag given Brennan's unhinged accusations on Twitter and his role promoting the Trump-Russia collusion fantasy.

While the name of the alleged whistleblower was a bombshell, Sperry's initial report contained other explosive revelations. It quoted an NSC source explaining why Ciaramella was removed from his White House gig. "He was accused of working against Trump and leaking against Trump." It also noted that Ciaramella worked with Alexandra Chalupa, the Ukrainian-American consultant for the Democratic National Committee who was a leading mudslinger of Russiagate dirt and baseless rumors. Chalupa, a Manafort-focused obsessive, met with Ciaramella at the White House as far back as 2015.[6]

These connections and rumors certainly merited disclosure and cast a shadow over the whistleblower's complaint. Many other curious connections and out-and-out disgraceful links have surfaced. And most of them could not have been established without knowing the alleged identity of Trump's accuser.

MORE CONNECTIONS

Alexandra Chalupa wasn't the only Democratic Party operative on Eric Ciaramella's contact list. In April 2016, around the time Trump had established himself as the probable Republican presidential nominee, longtime former Bill Clinton pollster Doug Schoen set up a meeting between Ciaramella and Ukrainian parliamentarian Olga Bielkova. At the time, Schoen was working as a lobbyist for Ukrainian billionaire Victor Pinchuk, whose estimated $10–25 million in donations to the Clinton Foundation have earned him the dishonor of being one of the top foreign contributors to Bill and Hillary's so-called charitable organization.

Schoen's Foreign Agent Registration filings reveal he arranged for Ciaramella and Liz Zentos, then NSC director for Eastern Europe, to meet with Bielkova "to discuss the Ukrainian progress in energy reform during the past year and what steps must be done in the future to increase energy independence and ensure energy security."

Later that day, Bielkova met with David Kramer of the McCain Institute. If the name Kramer sounds vaguely familiar, it should. He was the Johnny Appleseed of Christopher Steele's dossier of lies. Kramer was a trusted associate of John McCain. Just days after the 2016 election, he was approached by Sir Andrew Wood, the ex-British ambassador to Moscow, who knew about Steele's work. Kramer arranged a meeting with Wood and McCain. After being appraised of Steele's collection of collusion and creepy rumors, McCain dispatched Kramer to fly to Britain, meet Steele, and read the dossier. Returning to DC, Kramer picked up copies of the dossier from Glenn Simpson, showed one to McCain, and then began sharing the document with other government officials. Eventually, he also began sharing it with several reporters, including a scribe named Ken Bensinger who worked for Buzzfeed, the "news" site that published the entire unsubstantiated sleazy document for all the world to read.[7]

Bielkova's meeting with Kramer also reportedly concerned Ukraine energy reform. But it is remarkable that this Ukrainian politician would meet both Ciaramella and Kramer on the same day. If Ciaramella is indeed the whistleblower, Bielkova will have met with the two men who did more to spread anti-Trump propaganda than anyone this side of Glenn Simpson. And the meetings were brokered by Schoen, a Clinton pal who was being paid $40,000 to arrange meetings for Bielkova by Victor Pinchuk. (Actually, Schoen has been paid that monthly sum for years, according to FARA filings.)[8] But wait! It gets weirder. Pinchuk was a rabid supporter of Viktor Yanukovych, the former Ukraine president who installed Mykola Zlochevsky as his minister of ecology. Zlochevsky had another job, too. He was the president of Burisma—the troubled company that reportedly paid Joe Biden's son Hunter $83,333 per month for his "work" as a consultant and board member.[9]

Remember Obama's lawyer Greg Craig, one of the lobbyists who got caught in the Kyiv money swamp that I discussed in the opening chapter? Well, the money that got him investigated came from Victor

Pinchuk by way of Doug Schoen. You can read all about it in a registration statement filed on January 19, 2019, by the mighty law firm of Skadden, Arps, Slate, Meagher & Flom. It even notes, "The Firm understood that its work was to be largely funded by Victor Pinchuk," and lists Schoen and a company called Black Sea View Limited,[10] an enterprise controlled by Paul Manafort, as payors funneling funds from the Ukraine Ministry of Justice.[11]

I know. It's dizzying.

I have one more connection that should boggle your mind.

One of the main witnesses in the House impeachment hearings was David Holmes, a career diplomat who served as counselor for political affairs at the U.S. Embassy in Kyiv. Holmes, as you'll recall, made big headlines for testifying that he overheard a conversation between President Trump and Gordon Sondland, the millionaire hotelier turned United States ambassador to the European Union. Holmes claimed that during a July 26, 2019, outdoor lunch at a Kyiv restaurant with Sondland and two other staffers, the ambassador pulled out his cell phone and placed a call to the president. Trump was speaking so loudly, according to Holmes, that Sondland held the phone away from his ear, allowing his tablemates to hear the exchange.

Sondland then mentioned President Zelensky, Holmes testified, and Trump asked, "So he's going to do the investigation?"

"He's going to do it," Holmes recalled Sondland saying. Zelensky will "do anything you ask him to."[12]

After the phone conversation ended, Holmes testified that Sondland told him the president cared about "quote, unquote, 'big stuff' that benefits the President, like the quote, unquote 'Biden investigation.'"[13]

So that was career diplomat David Holmes's contribution to the hearings. Frankly, it made Sondland look like a bit of an idiot. Conducting national security business on an unsecured phone line in a public space should be a fireable offense at this point. Didn't he learn anything from the Mike Flynn investigation? Sondland confirmed the conversation took place but said he had no recollection of mentioning Biden. Curiously, although the House Democrats have scoured the earth for damning testimony, neither of the other two witnesses to this phone call has surfaced to corroborate Holmes's version of events. Why is that?

Holmes himself has some interesting connections. Or to be precise, his wife, Stephanie Holmes, does.

Stephanie Holmes, like her husband, is a career State Department employee. She also worked at the U.S. Embassy in Kyiv as director of the International Narcotics and Law Enforcement Affairs Office. But prior to that assignment, she worked in the National Security Council, where she was reportedly once accused of leaking details of Trump's Oval Office conversation with Russian Foreign Minister Sergei Lavrov and Russian Ambassador Sergey Kislyak. That Oval Office encounter took place on May 10, 2017, the day after Trump axed Jim Comey. The president reportedly told his guests that firing the "nut job" FBI director relieved "great pressure" on him. Subsequent reports suspiciously claimed Trump also shared critical, classified information about intelligence sources combating terrorism. According to the *Washington Post*, the suspicions surrounding Holmes over the leaks got so ugly, she even hired a lawyer. Eventually, she left the NSC for Ukraine.[14]

Stephanie Holmes, then, had a reason to resent the Trump administration. Her professional ties to the administration had thrown her career into temporary upheaval, which had presumably cost her money when she decided she needed to hire a lawyer. Do you think she resented Trump? Do you think, maybe, her husband might also have blamed the president for any "find-the-mole" pressure exerted on his wife? It is amazing to me that no one mentioned this incident to David Holmes during his testimony. As a witness, he presented himself as a rock-solid career diplomat. But if any of the people who testified against Trump at the impeachment hearings had a reason to be biased, Holmes fits the bill.

Stephanie Holmes also had a reason to be biased. We now know that even before Trump arrived at the White House, she was being fed anti-Trump emails by her friend Kathleen Kavalec, the deputy assistant secretary for the Bureau of European and Eurasian Affairs.

Kavalec met with Christopher Steele on October 11, 2016, and received a breathless briefing from the British fabulist. The veteran diplomat didn't buy everything Steele was trying to sell. As I noted in my previous book *Exonerated*, she immediately spotted a false detail in one of Steele's fabrications—a reference he made to a Russian consulate in Miami, which she knew didn't exist.

After her briefing from Steele, Kavalec sent a memo about his claims to several government agencies, including the FBI. While summarizing Steele's tale of a "technical/human operation run out of Moscow targeting the election" that recruited émigrés in the United States to "do hacking and recruitings," Kavalec also noted his false claim, but it's hard to give her a pass for that; she was spreading Steele's unsubstantiated, reckless garbage through the Obama administration.[15]

In three emails uncovered by a Freedom of Information Request, Kavalec forwarded articles that sounded alarm bells about Trump and Russia. On December 8, 2016, Holmes was one of three recipients of an email forwarding an article called "Trolling for Trump: How Russia Is Trying to Destroy Our Democracy." On February 9, 2017, Kavalec sent Holmes an article called "Reuters Exclusive: In Call with Putin, Trump Denounced Obama-Era Nuclear Arms Treaty." One day later, she forwarded the *Washington Post* article, "National Security Adviser Flynn Discussed Sanctions with Russian Ambassador, Despite Denials, Officials Say." All three articles touch on Trump and Russia, and none of them is flattering to the new administration. The first implies Russia is backing Trump. The second is about Trump confronting Russia on missiles, which goes against liberal doctrine, but it is also about Trump criticizing the Obama administration. The third alleges Trump's national security advisor consulted Ambassador Kislyak and then lied about it.[16]

Were these emails purely work-related? Or did Kavalec and Holmes harbor anti-Trump sentiments? Unfortunately, House investigators on both sides of the aisle failed to ask David Holmes about this issue as well.

SCHIFF'S INSIDER MOVES

From the moment the Democrats took the House in the 2018 election, Adam Schiff has been focused on investigating and convicting Donald Trump. In a December 2018 interview, as he was gearing up to become the chairman of the House Intelligence Committee, he was actively engaging in delusional conspiracy fantasies.

"At the end of the day, what should concern us most is anything that can have a continuing impact on the foreign policy and national-security policy of the United States, and, if the Russians were laundering money for the Trump Organization, that would be totally compromising," he said, speculating Trump would use the presidency to enrich himself. "There's a whole constellation of issues where that is essentially the center of gravity," Schiff said. "Obviously, that issue is implicated in efforts to build Trump Tower in Moscow. It's implicated in the money that Trump is bragging he was getting from the Saudis. And why shouldn't he love the Saudis? He said he was making so much money from them."[17]

Never mind that the Trump Organization was in the business of making money, or that the president had largely handed the reins of his business to his sons, or that Trump has spent his entire life talking up his achievements. Everything he did was, in Adam Schiff's eyes, something that "implicated" him.

Well, here is something that implicates Adam Schiff. Get ready.

In that same interview, while discussing his role of chairing one of the most powerful committees on Capitol Hill, Schiff bragged, "We've been deluged with résumés."[18]

And who, out of that flood of résumés, did Schiff and his committee hire?

Two pals of alleged whistleblower Eric Ciaramella!

I am not making this up.

The first hire was Abigail Grace, who worked at the National Security Council from 2016 to 2018 as a China expert. Evidently, her résumé rose quickly to the top of the pile; by early February, she was on the books and working to probe Trump's finances.

Six months later, another liberal NSC refugee arrived at the Schiff-run committee offices. His name was Sean Misko, and he had been director for the Gulf States at the Security Council. Schiff hired him on July 26, one day after Trump's call with Ukraine President Zelensky.[19]

According to reports, Misko and Ciaramella were pals at the NSC. They grabbed lunch together and commiserated about the policy shifts initiated by President Trump. An unnamed source told RealClearInvestigations that in 2017, he heard the two holdovers from the Obama NSC denouncing Trump's isolationist foreign policy. The source claimed the aides vowed to get rid of Trump.

Normally, I wouldn't put too much credence in this tale. The source wasn't named and this particular conversation—two mid-level NSC employees engaged in what passes for typical liberal wishful thinking—seems like it was just anti-Trump trash talk. In hindsight, however, the way events shook out makes their plotting sound completely plausible.

In August 2019, Misko's first month on the job, the whistleblower approached a House Intelligence Committee aide to voice his concerns about the president's call. An aide—it's not clear if it was Misko, Grace, or someone else—told the wannabe whistleblower "to find a lawyer to advise him and meet with an inspector general, with whom he could file a whistle-blower complaint," reported the *New York Times*. "The aide shared some of what the officer conveyed to Mr. Schiff. The aide did not share the whistle-blower's identity with Mr. Schiff."[20] Yeah. Sure.

This exchange is interesting because it provides clear proof that Adam Schiff, who presents himself as the tip of the spear of truth and justice, brazenly lied about what his committee knew about the whistleblower and when. On September 17, 2019, Schiff appeared on MSNBC and said, "We have not spoken directly with the whistleblower." Schiff also said, "We would like to, but I'm sure the whistleblower has concerns, that he has not been advised, as the law requires, by the inspector general or the director of national intelligence just as to how he is to communicate with Congress."

But that was a lie. A committee aide personally and directly gave the whistleblower directions on how to file his complaint and then briefed Schiff on the matter.

Now it turns out that two aides working for the committee knew the alleged whistleblower Ciaramella.

Schiff was playing his holier-than-thou, justice-warrior role to the hilt. And he was busted. Even liberal, and left-leaning, media outlets such as CNN and USA Today couldn't avoid blowing the whistle on Schiff.

But this wasn't the only time Schiff was posturing and hiding what he knew. In fact, the whistleblower reached out to him personally. Before we get to that, let's take a slight detour.

ATKINSON'S CONFLICT

Ciaramella isn't the only player in the Impeachment Implosion to have suspect connections. Inspector General Michael Atkinson, who legitimized the whistleblower complaint despite detecting "some indicia of an arguable political bias," may have had some issues of his own.

Before his position as the intel watchdog, he worked for former acting Assistant Attorney General Mary McCord. A longtime Department of Justice lawyer who headed the DOJ's National Security Division from October 2016 until April 2017, McCord helped oversee the corrupt FBI investigation into the Russian collusion hoax. She quit in 2017 to become the legal director at Georgetown University's Institute for Constitutional Advocacy and Protection. Why did the long-time department lawyer leave the DOJ at such a critical point? "I came to the conclusion that because I didn't feel that I could actively undermine policy decisions and other things that were being done, I needed to leave," she confessed during a 2018 panel discussion at the Brookings Institute.[21]

So unlike Ferrante and, allegedly, Ciaramella and Misko, McCord *claims* she was uncomfortable working against Trump from within his own administration. She claims she had standards, but we are all wondering where those standards were when she was waist-deep in the targeting of General Flynn, and the spying operation on the Trump team. Actively opposing and destroying Trump from across the aisle, however, was totally acceptable for McCord. She signed on to become a top outside counsel to support the impeachment effort and guide congressional Democrats as they battled to access documents and testimony. She also represented the Judiciary Committee in its fight to obtain Trump counsel Don McGahn's testimony and Mueller's grand jury evidence.

Given his previous close working relationship with McCord at the DOJ, shouldn't Atkinson have recused himself? Or at least bent over backward investigating the whistleblower's claims and motivations? It sure seems that way.

The president clearly thought so. On April 4, 2020, he notified Congress that Atkinson would be removed from his post within thirty days, effectively firing the compromised watchdog. "It is vital that I have the fullest confidence in the appointees serving as inspectors general," Trump wrote in a memo to Congress. "This is no longer the case with regard to this inspector general."[22]

At issue were three key decisions Atkinson made regarding the whistleblower complaint.

His first questionable decision was finding that the complaint met the standard of "urgent concern." The Intelligence Community Whistleblower Protection Act of 1998, or ICWPA, allows the intel community to share classified information with congressional intelligence committees if it is "an *urgent* concern."

The law defines this term as: "A serious or flagrant problem, abuse, violation of law or Executive order or deficiency *relating to the funding, administration, or operation of an intelligence activity within the responsibility and authority of the Director of National Intelligence* involving classified information but does not include differences of opinions concerning public policy matters." (Emphasis added.)

But the whistleblower's complaint had nothing to do with "funding, administration, or operation of an intelligence activity," as *The Federalist*'s Margot Cleveland has pointed out.[23] Instead, it asserted that Trump "sought to pressure the Ukrainian leader to take actions to help the President's 2020 election bid." That has nothing to do with an intelligence activity. But Atkinson, perhaps stealing a page from Sally Yates's playbook, justifies "urgent concern" by saying that if Trump did this, he might create "serious national security and counterintelligence risks."

The second misstep was his initial decision to deem the complaint "credible." As we know, several facts in the report were accurate. There was a call. Trump said what he said. And we now have the transcript. But the meaning and intent of the conversation are subject to interpretation. Also subject to interpretation, as I've mentioned, is what is permissible "diplomacy," what is commonsense relationship building, and what is the value of uncovering the suspicious activities of the Biden family in Ukraine? All these complex questions point to the complaint being ambiguous at best. And then there were the motives of the whistleblower, who, if it is Ciaramella, may have been driven by political bias. Despite all these known unknowns, Atkinson didn't bother accessing the actual call or transcript. He just asked staffers to investigate. "I decided that access to the records of the phone call was not necessary to make my determination that the complaint relating to the urgent concern 'appears credible,'" he wrote in his August 26 letter handing off the matter to then-Director of National Intelligence Joseph Maguire.[24] In other words, he opted not to verify what did or didn't happen during the Trump-Zelensky call in the Situation Room that was at the heart of the complaint, and just decided this "urgent concern" status was in the realm of believability because, well—just because it might be true.

(People tell themselves something similar every time they buy a lottery ticket: there's a chance you might win, right? Hey, I don't mind playing the lottery. But I'm not going to tell you it's a legit move to make some cash just because there's a tiny chance you might win.)

Atkinson then passed the complaint to then-Director of National Intelligence Joseph Maguire, which set the clock ticking. Maguire was legally bound to inform Congress of the complaint within seven calendar days. For his part, Maguire, citing concerns the complaint may have touched on issues covered by executive privilege, missed that deadline. On September 9, 2019, Atkinson informed the House and Senate intelligence committees that a whistleblower had filed a complaint.[25]

In doing so, Atkinson was disobeying instructions from the Department of Justice, according to Attorney General Bill Barr. "He was told this in a letter to the Department of Justice, and he is obliged to follow the interpretation of the Department of Justice, and he ignored it," Barr said.[26]

SCHIFF'S NEW GEAR

Atkinson's tip-off was just what Adam Schiff was waiting for. He had received the letter from the whistleblower back on August 12, the same day Atkinson got the complaint. He already knew about the allegations it made against the president. In fact, if you want to get technical about it, Schiff actually learned about the whistleblower's concerns *before the complaint was even filed.* Remember, Ciaramella, if it was him, approached a House Intelligence Committee aide to voice his concerns about the president's call and was told to find a lawyer and file a complaint. The aide told Schiff some of what the prospective whistleblower had conveyed, but apparently did not share the whistleblower's identity with the committee chairman.[27]

But now that Atkinson had informed the committee, Schiff had the cover he needed to launch the scandal into the national news cycle. On September 10, 2019, Schiff wrote and released a letter to Maguire that accused the head of National Intelligence of violating the law by not forwarding the complaint to Congress. In the process, he created a storyline that resounds with the Democrats' favorite fairy tales: obstruction and cover-up!

"Contrary to your express obligations under the law, you are withholding from the Committee an authorized and protected whistleblower disclosure involving 'a serious or flagrant problem, abuse, violation of law or Executive order…involving classified information.'"[28]

Democrats had tried to saddle Trump with obstruction charges frequently during Mueller's Russiagate witch hunts. Now Schiff resorted to the old playbook: "We do not know whether this decision to withhold the disclosure was made only by you or whether it involved interference from other parties including the White House." He also added the committee was concerned about "improper White House efforts to influence your office"—which is kind of ridiculous, considering Maguire was appointed by President Trump.

The deadline for getting the congressionally approved military aide to Ukraine was approaching. The day of Schiff's letter marked twenty days until the money earmarked for the Kyiv aid package would expire. On September 11, the package was released. Ukraine got the military aid it requested.

The timing was curious.

Did alleged whistleblower Ciaramella's complaint have anything to do with motivating the release of those funds?

Or should we conclude that Michael Atkinson's decision to legitimize the complaint was what got everyone's attention?

Or was it Atkinson's decision to go to Adam Schiff and provide him with a reason to write a public letter, suggesting there was yet another sky-is-falling plot and cover-up?

Or maybe the administration just did what the law said it had to do.

Once again, optics were poised to obscure the truth and fan liberal paranoia. The scandal the negative-spin masters of the Democratic Party, led by charlatan Adam Schiff, had fantasized about for three full years was unfolding before them. The impeachment onslaught was now in full effect. It had no chance of bearing fruit. The Republican-held Senate had zero intention of convicting a president for doing exactly what presidents are supposed to do.

But Adam Schiff and his cronies didn't care. They had a plan, a true vision to enact.

All that was left was to launch a nationally televised waste of time.

CHAPTER 9

The China Crisis—How Beijing Turned a Virus Into an Act of War

A merica is at war.

The COVID-19 virus has unleashed the most devastating attack on America in our nation's history. As I write this chapter, over one hundred thousand Americans have died. By the time this book is published, experts predict that number is likely to be two hundred thousand.

But we are not only at war with the virus.

We are at war with ourselves.

The fight over how to respond to the COVID-19 catastrophe has been politicized to toxic levels. Democrats accuse the Trump administration of failing to respond quickly—ignoring the onslaught of misinformation that came out of China and its puppet organization, the World Health Organization.

Is anyone surprised?

What should be a national tragedy that brings us together is instead pulling us apart. The airwaves and internet are filled with accusations, misinformation, and politicians on both sides playing their favorite blame games, as well as hot potato and pass the buck.

The result has been chaotic. The biggest economic meltdown in the history of our nation unfolded as a result. Forty million people lost their jobs.[1] Food lines and debt spread because of state-ordered shutdowns that purport to protect citizens' physical health but also put their fiscal health, and the now-struggling health care system, in danger. The Treasury has added trillions of dollars of debt to the national bottom line. It is a treacherous balancing act, and one that has our nation teetering on the brink of collapse.

Who benefits when America is destabilized?

Our rivals. Our enemies.

I'm not talking about political parties. I'm talking about *foreign entities*.

I'm talking specifically about China.

The intentions of the Chinese Communist Party (CCP) are going to be debated for years to come. But what cannot be debated is that the disease originated in or around Wuhan, China, and the CCP's efforts to not only cover up the disease, but also to spread it far and wide. The fact is—and I'm going to repeat this fact numerous times in this chapter, so get used to it—that on January 23, 2020, Wuhan went into lockdown and transportation from Wuhan to other parts of China was stopped, *but external flights from Wuhan Tianhe International Airport continued for days and days.* China was seeding the world with the virus—even though it was desperately trying to stop the spread of the dangerous virus among its own population.

This is not some half-baked conspiracy theory.

This is a fact.

A study by the University of Southampton noted that if China had instituted non-pharmaceutical intervention three weeks earlier, cases could have been reduced by 95 percent.[2] The tide would have turned. Containment might have been possible.

Instead, as a timeline in this chapter will show, China avoided publicizing the extent of the disease. It pressured the WHO to delay grave warnings. *It let the disease spread across the globe.*

Why would it do such a thing?

The short answer is that China is at war with us, too.

The longer answer involves digging into a little political history, including China's foreign policy and our own government's long-time, kid-gloves attitude toward our greatest rival. Then we can look at how China executed this crime against humanity—roping in the United Nations' primary global health-monitoring organization to help it dupe the world.

THE ORIGIN DEBATE

Soon after a coronavirus dubbed COVID-19 was identified as the mass killer rampaging through Wuhan and Hubei Province, reports began to surface that a local establishment, the Wuhan Institute of Virology (WIV), hosted several labs to study coronaviruses.

A January 19, 2018, State Department cable to Washington sounded the alarm about lab safety protocols at the institute after a U.S. delegation toured the facility. "During interactions with scientists at the WIV laboratory, they noted the new lab has a serious shortage of appropriately trained technicians and investigators needed to safely operate this high-containment laboratory," the worried diplomats wrote. They also reported researchers had been working with bats and that lab findings suggested "that SARS-like coronaviruses from bats can be transmitted to humans to cause SARS-like diseases. From a public health perspective, this makes the continued surveillance of SARS-like coronaviruses in bats and study of the animal-human interface critical to future emerging coronavirus outbreak prediction and prevention."

One of the WIV experts the American team met was scientist Shi Zhengli, who has been studying coronaviruses and bats for more than fifteen years. In 2017, her team concluded that horseshoe bats found in Yunnan Province were from the same bat population that had spawned the SARS coronavirus in 2003. With COVID-19, Shi's reams of information helped determine the deadly Wuhan coronavirus had also probably come from a similar animal. The new virus was a 96 percent match to a genetic sequence her team had found from a bat sample taken in 2013.

Given all these facts, you don't need to be a virologist, a doctor, or scientist to start asking the logical question. You just need common sense: Did COVID-19 come from the WIV lab?

And asking that question doesn't make you paranoid or a xenophobe. It is just a logical question. The origin story that has emerged from the beginning of the outbreak magically linked the virus to a "wet" market in Wuhan where wild animals were sold. But initial medical studies out of Wuhan never mentioned a wet market. They mentioned a *seafood market*. As in, *many of the initial forty-one victims were linked to a seafood market*. Are bats sold at seafood markets? I have no idea. There has also been speculation that the virus may have jumped from bats to humans via an intermediary animal, like a snake or pangolin, which are sold at these markets. Meanwhile, the earliest known patient in a study released in *The Lancet,* who surfaced with symptoms on December 1, had no connection to the seafood market, or to a so-called "wet" market.[3] At any rate, Wuhan clearly had a repository of bat virus at the Virology Institute. So, it is perfectly logical to wonder if a breach—which American officials had worried about two years earlier—occurred.

The line of the WIV has been, predictably, deny, deny, deny.

Shi told a local government newspaper she'd "guarantee on my life" that the virus hadn't come from her lab. Yuan Zhiming, WIV bigshot, declared, "There's no way this virus came from us."[4]

Of course, there are plenty of ways a virus could have made its way out of the Wuhan Institute of Virology. For all anyone knows, one of Shi's employees might be a homicidal maniac. Maybe a rat gnawed its way into a contaminated zone. But we don't need to resort to extraordinary leaps to explain this. Accidents happen. And CCP members lie.

U.S. intelligence analysts have been trying to determine if anything went terribly wrong at the institute. One report they have been studying, according to NBC News, determined that cell phone activity shut down in a high-security portion of the Wuhan Institute of Virology from October 7 through October 24, 2019. The report speculates that a "hazardous event" may have occurred sometime between October 6 and October 11.[5]

Intelligence analysts have been unable to conclusively verify the twenty-six-page document's conclusions. But we do know that early samples of the virus were intentionally destroyed. Liu Dengfeng, a National Health Commission official, has now confirmed Chinese authorities obliterated samples taken at the earliest stages of the outbreak—a charge issued by Secretary of State Mike Pompeo. Liu insists the action was taken to "prevent the risk to laboratory biological safety and prevent secondary disasters caused by unidentified pathogens."[6] But by getting rid of these key samples, China was ruining any chance of accurately tracking the evolution of the virus. So far, virology experts say there is no evidence the genetic sequence of the COVID-19 virus has been tampered with or weaponized for biowarfare. But who knows what those destroyed samples might have revealed.

Even if the virus didn't surface from the Wuhan Institute of Virology and it did, in fact, jump to humans because some moron ate a bat, nothing absolves the government of the Chinese Communist Party of its disgraceful behavior by suppressing information about the disease and then actively exporting a lethal virus. If anything, the presence of so much coronavirus research in Wuhan should have compelled authorities to be far more vigilant and responsive. That wasn't the case.

Why?

A GLOBAL BATTLE

For nearly fifty years, since Nixon went to China, America has gotten duped by Beijing.

As Brigadier General (Ret.) Robert Spalding says in his eye-opening book *Stealth War: How China Took Over While America's Elite Slept*, China has been playing a brilliant, simple-yet-sophisticated game, a "competition to gain control and influence across the planet and to achieve that outcome without resorting to military engagement."[7] To do that, China initially presented itself as an impoverished, backward nation with no plans for expansionism. Unlike the Soviet Union, it was not funding regimes in Afghanistan or Africa. It focused inward, trying to obtain technology and scientific knowledge. It sent students to study in American universities and work in labs. Gradually, China opened itself up to business, and America's academics and politicians deluded themselves into thinking that economic growth would magically lead to democratization. This delusion persisted after the world witnessed the 1989 Tiananmen Square massacre in which the CCP called in the People's Liberation Army—don't you love the irony of that name?—to crush a growing pro-democracy movement and slaughter its supporters.

American businesses and investors didn't blink. Lured by the slave-like wages they could pay Chinese laborers and the resultant increased profit margins, corporations moved operations to China's eager and accommodating cities. When Bill Clinton granted China most-favored-nation status and China was admitted into the World Trade Organization, the floodgates opened. No longer worried by potential import tariffs, American business and investment poured into China, turning the communist nation into the manufacturing capital of the entire world. It also became the piracy capital of the world and the technology theft capital of the world. It became common practice for the plans of American-designed products to be illegally copied so manufacturers could knock off exact, unlicensed copies at another factory. The

Chinese government has refused to crack down on piracy for decades. Technology acquisition by any means necessary—via cyberattacks, elaborate data theft operations, start-up acquisitions—has become a national obsession.

American cash and investment have always been welcome in China. The more the better for a nation that requires foreign reserves to pay for its vast energy needs—China is the number one importer of oil in the world—and relies on investment dollars and profits to lift its population up from widespread poverty. But American ideals—freedom of speech, freedom of the press, freedom of religion, freedom of movement and rule of law, and the idea that every citizen should have the protection of due process—have never been welcome. In fact, government edicts, like the infamous Document 9, have made it clear that the Chinese Communist Party regards these crucial American freedoms as a threat to its existence. Here's one excerpt from Document 9—the ninth paper issued in 2013 by the Central Committee of the Communist Party of China's General Office. Talk about paranoia:

> Western Constitutional Democracy has distinct political properties and aims. Among these are the separation of powers, the multi-party system, general elections, independent judiciaries, nationalized armies, and other characteristics. These are the capitalist class' concepts of a nation, political model, and system design....The point of publicly proclaiming Western constitutional democracy's key points is to oppose the party's leadership and implementation of its constitution and laws. Their goal is to use Western constitutional democracy to undermine the Party's leadership, abolish the People's Democracy, negate our country's constitution as well as our established system and principles, and bring about a change of allegiance by bringing Western political systems to China.[8]

In other words, individual rights are bad. The CCP is good.

Gradually, as China's economic power increased, its goals for global influence increased too. It has honed a two-tiered strategy in the world.

First, appear cooperative and positive at all times. Second, do whatever it takes to gain influence, even if it means breaking laws, abandoning ethics, and bribing world leaders. China has harnessed Western investment at every turn to use to its advantage, even floating a well-disguised $1 billion bond on Germany's Frankfurt Stock Exchange to fund the China Shipbuilding Industry Corporation, the company building China's first nuclear-powered aircraft carrier.[9]

China is a member of the World Trade Organization, but foreign-owned companies can't just open operations in China. They must have Chinese co-owners. And all companies must have a CCP representative on the board. Not only that, but *any profits earned in China must stay in China*. Repatriation of profits and investments is a long and difficult, if not impossible, process. How is that fair trade?

Foreign businesses keep opening in China because the amount of wealth there is massive and companies are fearful of missing out on obtaining critical market share. They believe they have to be in it to win it, and they hope that one day the rules will change and they can add their profits to the balance sheet back home.

As long as the CCP is in power, they can dream on.

Meanwhile, China has been consolidating power. It controls the world's manufacturing and supply chains. It exports its telecom systems throughout the world, giving it access to massive amounts of data that citizens transmit through cell phones—their location, their texts, emails, contacts, and images. This data fuels China's transformation into a dystopian surveillance state. And Chinese telecoms are offering a suite of tools to African nations allowing governments to spy on their people.[10]

Surveillance know-how aside, the one area that China has failed to dominate is the technology sphere. But the country has launched its Thousand Talents Program to lure American experts to come work in China. It sends thousands of STEM students to U.S. universities, where they can access research. It also issued two government visions for the future. The first is a ten-year plan called Made in China 2025 that will transform China into the dominant technology manufacturing power in ten high-tech spheres.[11] The second is the Belt and Road Initiative, a multibillion-dollar shipping network between China and the developing world that will, if it succeeds, give the CCP control of the flow of goods and data for 62 percent of the world's population and 75 percent of known energy reserves, according to strategy analysts and data from the World Bank.[12]

From Nixon to Carter to Clinton to Obama with the Bushes in between, no president has dared to call out China for its two-tiered system of rules. How it provides factories for the world, borrows cash, and floats bonds, but refuses to comply with the same finance laws everyone else does. The CCP prevents audits of its companies, won't stop piracy, demands technology transfer, sets the value of its own currency, and refuses to let profits leave the country. It seizes assets and transfers ownership on a whim. It demands access to foreign markets yet prevents access to its own.

But the free pass Clinton, Bush, and Obama gave to the CCP ended in 2016 with the election of Donald Trump.

As even a die-hard liberal I know admits, Trump is the first American president—the ONLY American president—with the guts to tell China that its scams have to stop. On August 14, 2017, Trump ordered the Office of the United States Trade Representative (USTR) to probe claims "China has implemented laws, policies and practices…that may encourage or require the transfer of American technology and intellectual property to enterprises in China or that may otherwise negatively affect American economic interests."

The USTR report was blistering. "Prior to 2001, China often explicitly mandated technology transfer…as a quid pro quo for market access," investigators noted. After joining the WTO, "China's technology transfer policies and practices have become more implicit, often carried out through oral instructions and 'behind closed doors.'"[13] This covert pressure was required because demanding technology for market access is a violation of the WTO agreement.

The report also noted ten or more instances when President Xi or other government representatives pledged to relax tech-transfer demands on American companies and guarantee that the CCP would not pressure anyone. Investigators, however, found no evidence this policy was ever formalized, much less enacted.

The Trade Representative's 182-page report is fascinating and frightening reading. It is also a major reason Trump decided that enough was enough.

Despite all the undeserved and manufactured attacks by the Deep State and Never-Trump maniacs in his administration, Donald Trump has not wavered on challenging and transforming China's trade tactics. In the summer of 2018, the president placed tariffs on over $250 billion of goods imported from China.[14] The message was clear to both Beijing and American corporations outsourcing to China: unless Beijing agreed to level the playing field and respect fair trade rules, Washington was going to put up barriers. Trump also initiated the U.S. withdrawal from the Universal Postal Union treaty, which underwrites the cost of international mail for developing countries. Since 1969, it cost less to ship a small package from Beijing to New York than it does to mail one from 1600 Pennsylvania Avenue to Congress. For decades, Chinese firms have shipped items via companies like Amazon and eBay to buyers in the U.S. It is estimated that billions of dollars' worth of pirated items—products invented by American companies—have been shipped and subsidized by the U.S. Postal Service which estimates it is losing $170 million annually on the Postal Treaty deal with China. This piracy-rewarding policy deprived our own companies of revenue they deserved and our treasury of taxes those revenues would have generated.[15]

The Trump administration has also worked actively to oppose China's dominance of 5G, the cutting-edge phone and data transmission network currently being implemented around the globe. Trump's team recognizes that Chinese telecoms like Huawei and others act hand-in-glove with the CCP. The installation and security around 5G networks are a national security issue not only for America but for our allies. Given China's obsession with data and surveillance, allowing Chinese firms to dominate this telecom sector risks exposing data, shredding privacy protections, and potentially ceding vital control of millions of digital machines and systems.

Add all this up, and Trump has become a major obstacle—arguably *the* major obstacle—in China's obsessive march to extend its totalitarian vision on the world. During Trump's tenure, China's explosive growth has slowed. Its debt-to-earnings ratio has grown wider. Trump has been an undeniable and unpredictable X factor.

Given all this, it is easy to imagine the CCP political and economic strategists running game theory simulations focusing on one thing: preventing Trump from winning the 2020 election. The CCP knows that Joe Biden would be a patsy for them. Obama refused to take any of the stop-China actions that Trump has. And Biden is even more clueless and easy to manipulate than his former boss. For one thing, as I reported in *Exonerated*, the Bank of China gifted a $1 billion investment fund to Hunter Biden and his pals back when Joe was in office as vice president. God and Beijing only know what kind of leverage the CCP is holding over that family. For another, Biden put his ignorance of China's sinister slow-play threat against America on full display while campaigning for the Iowa Caucus. There, clueless Joe was shocked at the mere suggestion China is our economic rival. "China is going to eat our lunch? Come on, man," the former vice president said.

"They can't figure out how they're going to deal with the corruption that exists within the system," Biden said of China. "I mean, you know, they're not bad folks, folks. But guess what? They're not competition for us."[16]

This quote alone must have had Xi breaking out the bottles of *baijiu* and Moët. And after he finished toasting Biden's idiotic remark, you can bet he ordered his minions to figure out how to help Biden win the Oval Office in 2020.

How would they do that? What would stop Trump, especially with the stock market hitting all-time highs? Financial stability has been one of the most reliable indicators of an incumbent's reelection chances. As James Carville, the man who engineered Bill Clinton's unseating of George H. W. Bush, famously said: "It's the economy, stupid." How could China wound the American economy in its signature style—influencing an outcome without being held responsible?

In January 2020, Beijing had its answer.

HIDE AND SNEAK

The COVID-19 virus had been circulating in Wuhan for weeks, if not months, when details of the outbreak began to leak out into the world.

Back in December, Wuhan doctors had spotted a disease that reminded them of SARS. One of them, a relatively young ophthalmologist named Li Wenliang, sent a WeChat message to a group of medical school alumni. Seven patients from a local seafood market were quarantined in his hospital fighting an illness that appeared to be SARS-like, he wrote.[17]

Free speech is not a right in China. Urging democratic reform or criticizing the Communist Party of China can result in long prison sentences. There's even a legitimate argument to be made that the CCP believes it owns all speech. Seriously. The government claims every piece of electronic data created within its borders is CCP property. That means every tweet or post, every like, every email, every photo created in China is owned by the government. It also means, theoretically, any computer program or app a business creates in China is also the property of the most dystopian totalitarian regime in the world, a surveillance state with an estimated half-a-billion cameras monitoring its citizens at every turn.[18]

It's no surprise, then, that Dr. Li's post came to the attention of local authorities who reportedly attempted to silence Li. Police showed up and warned him to "stop making false comments." He was investigated for spreading rumors. Li, whose wife was pregnant, didn't just have to worry about his patients and his wife battling a killer disease; he had to worry about his career and reputation as well as his own health.

Government authorities did not share Li's alarm, or if they did, they kept very quiet about it. In the modern globalized world, where trade and travel require the movement of millions of people across borders, public health officials from all nations generally use the World Health Organization (WHO) as a resource to share and disseminate outbreak information. The WHO is the Switzerland-based health wing of the United Nations. On the last day of 2019, Wuhan health officials finally notified the organization that a cluster of pneumonia cases of unknown origin had surfaced in Wuhan, a city of thirteen million people.

What forced China to share this information? It's a good question. The Chinese authorities weren't the only ones who noticed Dr. Li's post on WeChat; the Centers for Disease Control in Taiwan saw it, too, and it instantly set off alarm bells.

Taiwan had good reason to monitor outbreaks from China. The nation, less than one hundred miles off the coast of China, welcomes hundreds of weekly flights from the mainland that bring in two million people annually. It was rocked by the 2003 SARS outbreak that originated in China.

The next day, December 31, Taiwan's government took two urgent steps. First, it "sent an email to the International Health Regulations (IHR) focal point under the World Health Organization (WHO), informing WHO of its understanding of the disease and also requesting further information from WHO," according to a statement.[19] Second, it "activated enhanced border control and quarantine measures based on the assumption that human-to-human transmission was in fact occurring.

These measures included screening passengers on flights from Wuhan prior to disembarkation."

Taiwan's response to the COVID-19 threat has been, quite simply, astounding. Press conferences were held daily, while travelers from Wuhan were tested rigorously and their health was monitored. The country has avoided disaster. The response from the WHO to its early warning was not nearly as impressive.

Despite Taiwan's wording its alert with great care—the Taiwanese CDC says its email "took pains to refer to atypical pneumonia, and specifically noted that patients had been isolated for treatment" (that's shorthand alerting health professionals to the strong possibility of human-to-human transmission)—the WHO did not respond or relay a warning to other members.

David Lin, of the Taipei Representative Office in the United Kingdom, described the WHO's reaction this way:[20]

> The warning was not shared with other countries by the WHO because of its relationship with China. That error ultimately delayed the global response to the pandemic. The politics of pandemics, which exists inside the WHO as well as between states, should be unacceptable to any country that cares about public health.[21]

This is the first evidence that the WHO was playing politics with a disease outbreak. But there's more, and it is damning. Let's start with the most blatant piece of evidence, a January 14, 2020, tweet from the global health agency.

> Preliminary investigations conducted by the Chinese Authorities have found no clear evidence of human to human transmission of the novel #coronavirus (2019 -nCov) identified in #Wuhan #China.[22]

Incredibly, on this same date, "a technical lead for the response noted in a press briefing there may have been limited human-to-human transmission of the coronavirus," reports an undated entry on the WHO timeline.[23] That technical lead was Maria Van Kerkhove, an American epidemiologist. How does she explain this outrageous disconnect? "What is said publicly or what is said through Twitter is very different than what is discussed between our countries and collaborators. When you hear of a cluster of pneumonia, anyone in the infectious-disease community would be lying if they didn't say there could be human-to-human transmission. That's what we acted on."[24]

Excuse me? Is anybody with a functioning brain working in Geneva? Why should what is said publicly about a possible health emergency be any different from what is said privately? And who funneled a "no evidence of human to human transmission" to the public relations team that posted the tweet? It must have come from somewhere. Twitter is one of the fastest information relay systems in the world. Van Kerkhove's organization posted blatant misinformation: *"The Chinese Authorities have found no clear evidence of human to human transmission of the novel #coronavirus."* How this happened and why it happened have still not been answered. Meanwhile, Van Kerkhove is sticking to her implausible deniability defense: "It's important that we acted as we believed this virus would transmit, and that's exactly what we did. Can we do better? Always. But that's true for everyone, everywhere."

Someone needs to come clean here. How did the WHO team act as if it was worried about transmission if it downplayed human-to-human transmission on social media?

It's easy to think that the WHO should get a pass for relaying a 100 percent bogus cover-up message from "Chinese Authorities" and that I'm shooting the messenger by blaming the WHO. But given the history of WHO director-general Dr. Tedros Adhanom Ghebreyesus and China's well-documented strategy of seeking "soft power" by controlling UN organizations—by 2018, Chinese nationals led four UN specialized agencies: the Food and Agriculture Organization (FAO), the International Civil Aviation Organization (ICAO), the United Nations Industrial Development Organization (UNIDO), and the International Telecommunication Union (ITU).[25]

Traditionally, when outbreaks arise anywhere on the planet, the WHO sends a team of experts to evaluate the situation. This did not happen. Instead, according to the WHO website, it established an "IMST (Incident Management Support Team) across the three levels of the organization: headquarters, regional headquarters and country level, putting the organization on an emergency footing for dealing with the outbreak." Note that country level is a very general term—this is not the same thing as saying "we sent a team into Wuhan."

The first member of WHO leadership to arrive in China was Director-General Tedros, according to a scathing article in *Foreign Policy*.[26] He did not go to Wuhan; he went to Beijing for a January 28 meeting with Chinese President Xi Jinping. It is well-documented that Tedros (Ethiopians traditionally have personal names and take their fathers' personal name as their second name; meanwhile, in China family names come first) owes his job and allegiance to Xi and China. In fact, you could say he owes much of his career to kowtowing to Beijing. Prior to heading the WHO, Tedros was Ethiopia's health minister (2005–12). During his tenure, he covered up three cholera epidemics in his home country, according to Lawrence O. Gostin, the director of the O'Neill Institute for National and Global Health Law at Georgetown University.[27]

Gostin launched these charges as Tedros was running to lead the WHO out of concern the WHO "might lose its legitimacy" if its leader was involved in covering up epidemics.

"He had a duty to speak truth to power and to honestly identify and report verified cholera outbreaks over an extended period," Gostin said.[28]

Other medical experts speaking off the record confirmed they suspected Ethiopia of hiding outbreaks. Despite these concerns, Tedros received strong backing from China, which wrangled enough votes from other nations to defeat his main rival for the position, UK doctor David Nabarro, in the first-ever election of a WHO director-general. Why did China back Tedros? According to the *Wall Street Journal*, during the four years Tedros spent as Ethiopia's foreign minister, China established a beachhead in the Horn of Africa nation by investing in Ethiopia and lending it billions of dollars.[29]

"Shortly after winning his WHO election," China expert Lanhee Chen wrote in the *Journal*, "Mr. Tedros traveled to Beijing and lauded the country's health-care system: 'We can all learn something from China.'"[30]

China is a master of predatory lending and dressing up developmental aid packages into deals that are akin to international loan sharking. Since 2000, it has lent Ethiopia more than $12 billion. This generosity has a habit of coming with frightening tight strings attached. The president of Sri Lanka struck a massive deal with the CCP-owned China Harbor Engineering Company to build a multibillion-dollar deep-dredged Hambantota Port for his island nation. It may have seemed like a good idea at the time, but by 2017, Sri Lanka was swamped by debt from the deal. It gave up control of Hambantota and the surrounding fifteen thousand acres of land for ninety-nine years.

In China's hands, national debt becomes a manipulative tool. According to researchers at Germany's Kiel Institute, China has shifted into overdrive as an international lender, handing out the bulk of an estimated $520 billion in loans to developing nations in the past twenty years.[31] That astounding figure makes China a bigger creditor than the World Bank. The CCP can use all its debt receipts to pressure countries in various ways. It can demand ownership of resources. It can forgive debt for favors, like casting votes in UN elections. And, as it did with Tedros, it can demand the head of an international agency send a message that will ultimately cripple its main rival's economy.

HOW TO CREATE AN INTERNATIONAL PANDEMIC AND A FISCAL MELTDOWN

The timeline of statements from Tedros and his organization suggest two possibilities. Either the WHO is grossly incompetent or it was manipulated by China. I believe both options are true. Here's a timeline of events:

December 1, 2019—The earliest known case of COVID-19 presents itself in Wuhan. (There has been one published report of a fifty-five-year-old from Hubei Province coming down with the disease on November 17, but this has not been confirmed.)

December 27, 2019—Dr. Zhang Jixian of Hubei Provincial Hospital of Integrated Chinese and Western Medicine tells China's health authorities that the disease was caused by a new coronavirus.[32]

December 30, 2019—Dr. Li posts his concerns of a coronavirus on WeChat.

December 30, 2019—Taiwan sends an email alerting the WHO of a possible coronavirus.

December 31, 2019—China finally informs the WHO of the outbreak.

January 12, 2020—China publicly shares the genetic sequence of COVID-19.

January 13, 2020—Thailand reports the first recorded case of COVID-19 outside China.

January 14, 2020—WHO tweets that authorities do not believe there was human-to-human transmission. *On this same day,* the WHO technical lead for the response tells the press that "there may have been limited human-to-human transmission of the coronavirus."

January 20–21, 2020—WHO experts from its China and Western Pacific regional offices conduct a brief field visit to Wuhan, apparently for the first time since the outbreak.

January 22, 2020—WHO bows to pressure from China, which the organization refers to as "divergent views," and refuses to issue a declaration of an International Public Health Emergency.

January 23, 2020—Officials in Wuhan issue a complete travel ban within the city.

January 25, 2020—All of Hubei Province is locked down.

January 25, 2020—Domestic flights within China from Hubei are stopped.[33]

January 30, 2020—The WHO's Emergency Committee (EC) convenes in Geneva and *finally* agrees that the outbreak now meets the criteria for a Public Health Emergency of International Concern.[34] *The organization reports there are cases in eighteen countries outside China.*

January 31, 2020—Trump issues a proclamation suspending the U.S. entry of all aliens who have been in China (excluding Hong Kong and Macau) within fourteen days of arrival.[35]

January 31, 2020—Italy bans all flights to and from China.

February 1, 2020—China's Vice-minister of Foreign Affairs Qin Gang meets the Italian Ambassador to Beijing to complain about the ban. The Chinese foreign ministry gets in on the act, whining that the move has "caused great inconvenience to citizens of both countries. Many Chinese are still stranded in Italy."[36]

February 7, 2020—Coronavirus whistleblower Dr. Li dies of COVID-19, leaving behind his young son and pregnant wife.

March 1, 2020—The U.S. reports its first fatality from COVID-19, a man in Washington State in his fifties.

This timeline could go on and on. And yes, I've left out plenty of highlights about COVID-19's devastating migration. But its main goal was to show just how destructive China and the WHO were, how they acted in concert, and how their delays allowed the disease to spread and detonate a cataclysmic global health and economic crisis. The experts were completely alarmed, yet they failed to communicate the threat to the world.

Any doubt about whether Tedros was in the pocket of China became crystal clear to infectious disease experts—and anyone with half a brain—when, on February 3, the most powerful man in international disease control declared that no one needed to take steps that "unnecessarily interfere with international travel and trade."

At that point, the disease had killed hundreds, if not thousands, in China. And most importantly—I can't stress this enough—*China had banned internal travel and trade with the entire Hubei Province.* The totalitarian government was keeping sixty million of its citizens in absolute, total lockdown. It was sealing itself off from Hubei to protect itself from the killer virus. But Tedros's message to the rest of the world was: *don't ban travel and trade from China.* There are no words to describe this level of butt-kissing and sucking up by the leader of an international agency to its master. If an internal ban was needed to protect Beijing, it should have been extended to the rest of the world.

Why would Tedros deliver this advertisement for business as usual with Beijing? Because Beijing needs foreign trade for its massive, impoverished population. It needs dollars to meet its energy needs and to pay off its massive credit bills. Without trade, without manufacturing, the

CCP-controlled economy risked collapse. So Tedros actively went out and did China's bidding—issuing what we now know was insane advice.

A minimum of 430,000 people traveled from China to the U.S. from January 1 to early April. In the first half of January, four thousand travelers flew directly from Wuhan to American airports, a Chinese aviation data company told the *New York Times*. During January, 381,000 passengers flew into U.S. airports from China.[37] Meanwhile, the head of the World Health Organization was acting like this was no big deal.

THE DEADLY EXPORT

I know that I have advocated lifting the lockdown on my podcast. I support a focused, cautious opening up of society and our economy. People have to work. COVID-19 is a brutal killer that must be taken seriously. It kills a segment of the population with ruthless efficiency. I get it. But the economic devastation caused by the closing of American society has enormous costs to life, too. The fiscal crunch of the lockdown will destroy lives. We've seen this. Domestic abuse has skyrocketed, according to media reports. Alcoholism and drug abuse have also soared. The stress of a lockdown is enormous and the psychological and emotional costs are very real. Our food supply was strained, and many of our hospitals may be teetering on bankruptcy because of the ban on elective procedures.

The Chinese Communist Party knew all this before anyone. It had experienced the crippling COVID-19 effect. That's why the CCP activated its personal propaganda peon—Tedros, who did its bidding and delayed the WHO from classifying the Wuhan virus as a pandemic. Donald Trump's attacks on China and its WHO clown Tedros have been absolutely accurate. China and the WHO failed to protect the world. Millions will die. Billions will suffer from economic hardship.

On May 18, 2020, President Trump sent a letter to Tedros detailing many of the points I've laid out here. But he also included a shocking new allegation, apparently based on Dr. Yong-Zhen Zhang's article in the journal *Cell*, revealing that Zhang had sequenced the COVID-19 virus on January 5 and forwarded it to Chinese authorities, who failed to post the vital research, until Zhang posted it himself on January 11.[38]

After cataloguing nearly four pages of China-backed WHO failures in his letter, Trump laid it on the line: "The only way forward for the World Health Organization is if it can actually demonstrate independence from China," Trump wrote, giving Tedros thirty days to "commit to substantial improvements" or face the permanent loss of U.S. funding.[39]

Given the WHO's performance and China's manipulation of Tedros, it is hard to argue with Trump's stance. No wonder Trump decided to ignore his own deadline and announced on May 29 that he would cut ties to the organization.

The only remaining question, looking at China's behavior, is when and why Beijing decided to weaponize and export this disease. Seriously, the WHO has praised China for releasing the genetic code of the virus—which we know China stalled on releasing. But all of this is straight out of the CCP misdirection playbook. They appeared to be helping the world while they were actively working to hurt it.

Many readers are probably asking, why would China want to see the disease spiral out of control? Why, if America is such an important part of China's economy, would it want to damage our economy?

Let's return to my earlier points. China has been playing a long game. It always plays the long game. For fifty years, it has been slow-playing Washington. Donald Trump has finally called their bluffs—or, more accurately, their cheating ways. This has forced China to recalibrate its strategy.

I believe removing Trump has become an obsession in Beijing. To do that, CCP analysts realized that hurting the economy was the most efficient way of dismantling Trump's chance of reelection. While destroying the U.S. economy will hurt China, remember, the CCP is all about distant outcomes. They did the math. And they concluded that one year of fiscal damage would be nothing compared to four more years of

Trump dismantling Beijing's long-term plans. If they could help clueless Joe Biden win, they would have a useful idiot in charge—someone on record as thinking China is utterly harmless.

As this chapter has made clear, they are anything but.

The damage China has inflicted on the U.S. outstrips anything we've ever seen. The deaths and financial cost we've experienced have already surpassed World War I, the Korean War, and Vietnam put together. As China experts like General Spalding have revealed, China's strategy is to wage war and win without firing a single bullet.

Already experts in data theft, technology theft, and financial manipulation, China has just added a new element of warfare. The strategists of Beijing realized COVID-19 doesn't just kill people, it kills economies, too. Once the outbreak surfaced and escaped, Beijing pivoted. It pressured the WHO to soft-pedal the threat, buying time for the virus to spread, calculating that it would destroy the U.S. economy and, with that, Donald Trump's reelection chances.

The damage would be enormous. But the mortal threat to Beijing's master plan for world dominance would be removed.

CHAPTER 10

Making and Breaking the Connections

There is no magic bullet to solve the mountain of political problems America is facing.

Putting our faith in politicians is a hard thing to ask anyone. These are the very people who have voted for the abusive Patriot Act, sponsored endless foreign interventions with little to show for it, and swelled our national debt. As I've been known to say on my podcast, Republicans are probably not the answer to all our glaring problems, but Democrats are definitely the cause of them.

So, putting your faith in politicians can feel like worshipping golden-calf-like false idols, and sometimes our election options don't make things any easier. For years, I've felt like the people running for office frequently didn't understand or reflect my views and values. I was forced time and again to vote not for the good option, but for the less-bad option. The frustration I felt at the voting booth led me to run for office. I worked hard, but I was unsuccessful. Then I decided to agitate from outside the swamp rather than infiltrate it.

I am a Republican because I support the American ideals of freedom, liberty, privacy, security, and the pursuit of happiness. And because I don't think capitalism is a dirty word. I embrace it, and the risks and responsibilities that come attached to it.

But not every Republican is a hero.

Many of the outrageous stories that unfolded in this book occurred because of two-party complicity. Because people—many of them Republicans—failed to hold the line and prevent abuses of power set in motion by Democratic operatives. John McCain, a GOP stalwart, and his trusted aide David Kramer helped spread the salacious Steele dossier.

Robert Mueller—the former, "legendary" FBI director who continued the unprecedented assault on the presidency for more than two years as special counsel—is a Republican. So is the man who appointed and guided Mueller's multimillion-dollar witch hunt, Rod Rosenstein. And so, for most of his life, was FBI director and professional Trump-trapper James Comey. Yet that unholy trinity unleashed a war against the presidency that still has the nation reeling.

Malfeasance—the wrongful exercise of lawful authority—became a defining characteristic of the Obama administration and the anti-Trump cabal that arose in its wake. The impeachment charade was a stunning waste of time. A scandal manufactured by parsing the words of the president in the most negative light possible, which launched the unjustified case against Trump and paralyzed our government for over two months. Why? So Adam Schiff could get airtime on CNN and MSNBC and pitch his absurd fables? And because the Democrats thought that even if their fiasco failed, it would hurt the administration and the Republican's 2020 election chances.

What a noble cause, right?

Too many Republicans have toed the line in the last four years. If we knew the collusion allegations were nothing more than a hoax and if we knew the impeachment charges were bogus (and we did), then why didn't Republicans fight back harder? Bill Barr's reexaminations of the

Russiagate investigation have revealed prosecutorial abuses of power that should never have been tolerated.

But it's not easy. Time and again, the mainstream media bought what the leakers of the CIA, FBI, and DOJ were spouting. What Democrat-funded operatives like Glenn Simpson and Christopher Steele were marketing to anyone who would listen. What paid informant Stefan Halper seems to have fabricated out of nothing more than a chance dinner party meeting. The press repeated this innuendo and misinformation both fast and frequently.

Ironically, they missed reporting the truth about Donald Trump. They were so busy reporting that the sky was falling that they missed the revolution unfolding before their eyes. They couldn't understand that American voters admired his authentic maverick ways. Trump wasn't beholden to the Beltway elite or the Silicon Valley billionaires or old money special interest lobbies. He didn't need anyone for fame or fortune. He didn't need the money; he was already a millionaire. He didn't need the notoriety; he was already a household name. And he didn't cause the swamp chaos, because he was the cavalier outsider who was going to change it.

He wasn't the lesser of two options (how could you be less than Hillary Clinton?), he was a completely new option: an unapologetic American, unafraid to speak his mind.

The media was so blind to the appeal of this dynamic, so uncomprehending, that all the editors and scribes reacted as if it must be a devious plot. The worldview of these media milquetoasts is shaped exclusively within the Amtrak corridor, so this is the only possible way they could process these events. They had no frame of reference. And when the Never-Trumpers and Obamacrats began feeding them conspiracy tidbits, they vigorously ate it up. They thought they were white knights on a mission to save Democracy.

In reality, it was a misguided, desperate mission to save the Democratic Party.

Meanwhile, they failed to understand that nearly half the country saw Trump as the white knight.

In a sense, I am part of the media. So, I don't want to completely annihilate all my colleagues. But many deserve the abuse. They have failed to recognize the hypocrisy and double standards that lurked within almost every scandal that has threatened to engulf Trump. And they have helped perpetuate these double standards.

Paul Manafort took money from a Ukrainian billionaire and failed to register as a foreign agent? True. But Greg Craig and Tony Podesta reportedly took money from some of the same Ukrainian operatives as Manafort and also failed to register as foreign agents! Podesta walked away unscathed. Craig beat the charge against him. How? Why? Where was the unbridled outrage? Where were the articles in the mainstream press about Democratic power brokers being corrupt, greedy, and dirty?

Donald Trump asked a Ukrainian leader for a favor during a phone call? Well, Joe Biden has admitted to asking for a big favor—explicitly tying the removal of a Ukrainian prosecutor, who was investigating the company his son was working for, to a $1 billion loan. Not only that, why wasn't he prosecuted? No wonder Trump wanted Ukraine to investigate this malfeasance.

Michael Flynn has been dragged over the coals again and again, accused of lying to the FBI. I don't believe he lied—I think some of the details of his call got fuzzy while on vacation in the Dominican Republic. But Andrew McCabe, the FBI deputy director, was found to have repeatedly lied about leaking information to the *Wall Street Journal* about McCabe's role in the FBI's Clinton Foundation investigation. By authorizing the leak, McCabe basically confirmed an FBI probe—which, of course, is against bureau policy. Or, as Inspector General Michael Horowitz put it in his report on McCabe's role, he "lacked candor, including under oath, on multiple occasions in connection with describing his role in connection with a disclosure to the WSJ, and that this conduct violated FBI Offense Codes 2.5 and 2.6."[1]

Was Andrew McCabe prosecuted? Of course not. His attorneys got a nice letter—a valentine on Valentine's Day—from the DOJ's Fraud and Public Corruption Section informing them that "after careful consideration, the Government has decided not to pursue criminal charges against your client Andrew G. McCabe."[2]

McCabe lied and spun. He's been following the money, too—rewarded with a major book deal and a contract to work as a CNN contributor. Down is up, apparently, where Deep State actors are involved.

And yet Mike Flynn, as of this writing, was still trapped in legal limbo, being toyed with by an out-of-control federal judge. I pray he is finally exonerated.

This just doesn't make any sense. The same rules have to apply to both sides.

As frustrating as this situation is, I am not consumed by despair. In fact, I have hope. I'm forty-five years old, and I've lived through two impeachments, 9/11, the multibillion-dollar Iraq fiasco, eight years of Obama hell, four years of takedown attempts on Trump, the coronavirus plague, *and the biggest financial and employment meltdown since the Depression.*

And guess what? Despite all that—and despite the obvious bipartisan weaknesses of our political parties and our biased media infrastructure—we are still the land of the free. Basic individual freedoms still exist. Unlike in China, our citizens can say what we want, pray to whatever god we worship, think what we want, and print what we want. And we still have the greatest entrepreneurs and technology development on the planet. We remain the nation that the world flocks to. Nobody is trying to sneak into China for a better life. In fact, for the last two decades, the Chinese have spent billions of dollars annually to send hundreds of thousands of their kids to American universities for full, four-year and graduate programs. None of these kids are coming here on a semester abroad, a one-shot deal. By comparison, how many American high schoolers do you think are enrolling in four-year programs at Hubei State?

THE NEXT HURDLE

There is great uncertainty in the world as we address the issues of combatting the Wuhan, China, virus. But American exceptionalism isn't over. I believe it is coming back. There are things we need to do—ensure better civic education for our kids, elect better people, and stop China's slow-play anti-American offensive.

To do that, we need to pay close attention to the primaries and the candidates we are fielding. But think of what we've just endured. We have survived three-and-a-half years of manufactured scandals, of active measures against our own people, of relentless prosecutorial overreach. And Trump is still standing and fighting.

Voters need to remember how we got to Donald Trump. We have to pick candidates who aren't compromised by big-money interests, who aren't putting their personal gain first, who aren't going to create a monolithic big government, and who understand the importance of American freedoms.

We've just witnessed four years of spying on Trump. We've witnessed an unending, elaborate, three-part plot to target General Mike Flynn. As a former federal agent, I never thought I would see cases in this country where patriots are targeted because they challenge the orthodox power structures. The harassment and targeting that have occurred are the kinds of things that happen in third-world dictatorships. I can understand if this happens in a developing country, but not in America.

I have followed the money, the connections, the plots. I have laid out the abuses of power, the influence of billionaires, the targeting, and the conspiracies to manufacture conspiracies. But I can only do so much.

Now it is your turn to help take our country back.

ENDNOTES

CHAPTER 1

[1] Office of the Inspector General, *Review of Four FISA Applications and Other Aspects of the FBI's Crossfire Hurricane Investigation*, Department of Justice, December 2019, viii–xii. https://oig.justice.gov/reports/2019/o20012.pdf.

[2] Ibid., vi.

[3] "Transcript: Marie Yovanovitch's Nov. 15 Testimony in Front of the House Intelligence Committee," *Washington Post*, November 16, 2019, https://www.washingtonpost.com/politics/2019/11/16/transcript-marie-yovanovitchs-nov-testimony-front-house-intelligence-committee/.

[4] "Transcript: Fiona Hill and David Holmes Testimony in Front of the House Intelligence Committee," *Washington Post*, November 21, 2019, https://www.washingtonpost.com/politics/2019/11/21/transcript-fiona-hill-david-holmes-testimony-front-house-intelligence-committee/.

[5] Ibid.

[6] "Transcript: Vindman and Williams Testify in Front of the House Intelligence Committee on Nov. 19," *Washington Post*, November 19, 2019, https://www.washingtonpost.com/politics/2019/11/19/transcript-vindman-williams-testify-front-house-intelligence-committee-nov/.

[7] Glenn Simpson and Peter Fritsch, *Crime in Progress: Inside the Steele Dossier and the Fusion GPS Investigation of Donald Trump* (New York: Random House: 2019), 45.

[8] Andrew E. Kramer, Mike McIntire, and Barry Meier, "Secret Ledger in Ukraine Lists Cash for Donald Trump's Campaign Chief," *New York Times*, August 14, 2016, https://www.nytimes.com/2016/08/15/us/politics/what-is-the-black-ledger.html.

[9] Ibid.

[10] Sergii Leshchenko, "Sergii Leshchenko: The True Story of Yanukovych's Black Ledger," *Kyiv Post*, November 24, 2019, https://www.kyivpost.com/article/opinion/op-ed/sergii-leshchenko-the-true-story-of-yanukovychs-black-ledger.html.

[11] Ibid.

[12] John Solomon, "Key Witness Told Team Mueller That Russia Collusion Evidence Found in Ukraine Was Fabricated," Just the News, February 23, 2020, https://justthenews.com/accountability/political-ethics/key-witness-told-team -mueller-russia-collusion-evidence-found.

[13] Ibid.

[14] Richard Levick, "FARA's New 'Sheriff' Means Business," *Forbes*, September 26, 2019, https://www.forbes.com/sites/richardlevick/2019/09/26/faras-new-sheriff-means-business/#6607fe0153ad.

[15] Devlin Barrett and Spencer S. Hsu, "Former Trump Campaign Official Rick Gates Pleads Guilty to 2 Charges," *Washington Post*, February, 23, 2018, https://www.washingtonpost.com/politics/former-trump-campaign-official-rick-gates-expected-to-plead-guilty-and-cooperate-with-special-counsel-in-probe-of-russian-election-interference/2018/02/23/ceaaeac8-16b4-11e8-b681-2d4d462a1921_story.html.

[16] Special Counsel Robert S. Mueller III, *Report on the Investigation into Russian Interference in the 2016 Presidential Election, March 2019, Vol. 1*, p. 129.

[17] Ibid., 131.

[18] United States of America v. Paul J. Manafort, Jr. and Richard W. Gates III, 1:17-cr-00201-ABJ (US District Court for the District of Columbia, October 27, 2017), https://www.justice.gov/file/1007271/download.

[19] Michael T. Kaufman, *Soros: The Life and Times of Messianic Billionaire* (New York: Alfred A. Knopf, 2002), 170–171.

[20] Kenneth P. Vogel, Scott Shane, and Patrick Kingsley, "How Vilification of George Soros Moved from the Fringes to the Mainstream," *New York Times*, October 31, 2018, https://www.nytimes.com/2018/10/31/us/politics/george-soros-bombs-trump.html.

[21] "Democracy Integrity Project: Full Text of 'Form 990'" for Fiscal Year Ending Dec. 2017," Propublica, https://projects.propublica.org/nonprofits/organizations/815223488/201843199349303694/IRS990.

[22] Simpson and Fritsch, 172.

[23] Kenneth P. Vogel, "Russia Scandal Befalls Two Brothers: John and Tony Podesta," *New York Times,* November 10, 2017, https://www.nytimes.com/2017/11/10/us/politics/john-tony-podesta-mueller-russia-investigation.html.

[24] Letter from Matthew T. Sanderson to Heather Hunt of FARA Registration Unit, "RE: Reclassification of the Podesta Group's Prior Disclosure Act Registration for Former Client European Centre for a Modern Ukraine," April 12, 2017, https://secure.politico.com/f/?id=0000015b-6331-db04-ad5b-7bb9804c0000.

[25] Spencer S. Hsu and Rosalind S. Helderman, "Gregory Craig Found Not Guilty of Lying to Investigators Probing Work to Aid Ukraine President," *Washington Post*, September 4, 2019, https://www.washingtonpost.com/local/legal-issues/greg-

ory-craig-found-not-guilty-of-lying-to-investigators-probing-work-to-aid-ukraine-president/2019/09/04/b1273304-cf26-11e9-b29b-a528dc82154a_story.html.

26 "Fact Sheet: Open Society Foundations in Ukraine," Open Society Foundations, January 28, 2020, https://www.opensocietyfoundations.org/newsroom/the-open-society-foundations-in-ukraine.

27 James Marson and Brett Forrest, "Ukrainian Corruption Showdown Sets Stage for Impeachment Inquiry," *Wall Street Journal*, November 12, 2019, https://www.wsj.com/articles/ukrainian-corruption-showdown-sets-stage-for-impeachment-inquiry-11573605386.

28 "Foreign Affairs Issue Launch with Former Vice President Joe Biden," Council on Foreign Relations, January 23, 2018, https://www.cfr.org/event/foreign-affairs-issue-launch-former-vice-president-joe-biden.

29 Matthew Kupfer, "Ukrainian MP Releases Biden-Poroshenko Call Recordings, Spouts Absurd Conspiracy," *Kyiv Post*, May 19, 2020, https://www.kyivpost.com/ukraine-politics/ukrainian-mp-releases-biden-poroshenko-call-recordings-spouts-absurd-conspiracy-theory.html.

30 Office of the White House, "Readout of Vice President Biden's Call with President Petro Poroshenko of Ukraine," March 22, 2016, https://obamawhitehouse.archives.gov/the-press-office/2016/03/22/readout-vice-president-bidens-call-president-petro-poroshenko-ukraine.

31 Kupfer.

32 Paul Sonne and Rosalind S. Helderman, "Ukrainian Lawmaker Releases Leaked Phone Calls of Biden and Poroshenko," *Washington Post*, May 19, 2020, https://www.washingtonpost.com/national-security/ukrainian-lawmaker-releases-leaked-phone-calls-of-biden-and-poroshenko/2020/05/19/cc1e6030-9a26-11ea-b60c-3be060a4f8e1_story.html.

33 Letter from George Kent to Yuriy Stolyarchuk, April 4, 2016, https://www.scribd.com/document/402559592/Embassy2GPLetter4-4-16.

34 John Solomon, "Top Ukrainian Justice Official Says US Ambassador Gave Him a Do Not Prosecute List," The Hill, March 20, 2019, https://thehill.com/hilltv/rising/434875-top-ukrainian-justice-official-says-us-ambassador-gave-him-a-do-not-prosecute.

35 Ibid.

36 John Solomon, "US Embassy Pressed Ukraine to Drop Probe of George Soros Group during 2016 Election," The Hill, March 26, 2019, https://thehill.com/opinion/campaign/435906-us-embassy-pressed-ukraine-to-drop-probe-of-george-soros-group-during-2016.

37 Solomon, March 20, 2019.

38 Solomon, March 26, 2019.

39 Christian Oliver, "Save Ukraine to Counter Russia, Soros Says," *Financial Times*, January 7, 2015, https://www.ft.com/content/4ddfb410-9664-11e4-a40b-00144fe-abdc0.

40 "CLC Complaint Results in Arrest of Two Ukrainian-American Trump Donors Connected to Giuliani," Campaignlegal.org, October, 10, 2019, https://campaign legal.org/press-releases/clc-complaint-results-arrest-two-ukrainian-american-trump-donors-connected-giuliani.

41 John Solomon, "Latvian Government Says It Flagged 'Suspicious' Hunter Biden Payments in 2016," John Solomon Reports, December 17, 2019, https://johnsolomonreports.com/latvian-government-says-it-flagged-suspicious-hunter-biden-payments-in-2016/.

42 Ibid.

43 Joe Schoffstall, "Soros Bankrolls Coronavirus Attack Ads Against Trump," Washington Free Beacon, March 24, 2020, https://freebeacon.com/2020-election/soros-bankrolls-coronavirus-attack-ads-against-trump/.

44 "Receipts: Democracy PAC," Federal Election Commission Campaign Finance Database, FEC.gov, https://www.fec.gov/data/receipts/?data_type=processed&committee_id=C00495861&contributor_name=democracy+PAC&two_year_transaction_period=2020.

45 Daria Kaleniuk, "Ukraine Continues to Fight Corruption—Don't Believe the Smear," The Hill, April 2, 2019, https://thehill.com/opinion/international/436954-ukraine-continues-to-fight-corruption-dont-believe-the-smear.

46 AntAC home page, https://antac.org.ua/en/about-us/.

47 Sara Carter, "Whistleblower and DNC Contractor Visited Obama WH. It Must Be Investigated," Saracarter.com, November 8, 2019, https://saraacarter.com/whistleblower-and-dnc-contractor-visited-obama-wh-it-must-be-investigated.

CHAPTER 2

1 Jo Becker, Matt Apuzzo, and Adam Goldman, "Trump Team Met with Lawyer Linked to Kremlin During Campaign," *New York Times*, July 8, 2017, https://www.nytimes.com/2017/07/08/us/politics/trump-russia-kushner-manafort.html.

2 Matt Apuzzo, Jo Becker, Adam Goldman, and Maggie Haberman, "Trump Jr. Was Told in Email of Russian Effort to Aid Campaign," *New York Times*, July 10, 2017, https://www.nytimes.com/2017/07/10/us/politics/donald-trump-jr-russia-email-candidacy.html.

3 Donald Trump Jr. and Rob Goldstone, "Read the Emails on Donald Trump Jr.'s Russia Meeting," *New York Times*, July 11, 2017, https://www.nytimes.com/interactive/2017/07/11/us/politics/donald-trump-jr-email-text.html.

4 Ibid.

5   Sam Sifton, "Restaurant Review: Nello," *New York Times*, April 13, 2010, https://www.nytimes.com/2010/04/14/dining/reviews/14rest.html.

6   "Interview of Anatole Samochornov on 07/12/2017," Special Counsel Mueller Investigation Records Part 04, https://vault.fbi.gov/special-counsel-mueller-investigation-records/special-counsel-mueller-investigation-records-part-04-of-06/view.

7   Ibid., 54

8   Brendan Pierson, "U.S. Judge Orders Russian-Owned Company to Pay $6 Million Settlement," Reuters, March 2, 2018, https://www.reuters.com/article/us-usa-russia-prevezon/u-s-judge-orders-russian-owned-company-to-pay-6-million-settlement-idUSKBN1FM2FJ.

9   "Russian Lawyer Had Deep Ties to Kremlin, Emails Show," MSNBC, April 27, 2018,https://www.msnbc.com/rachel-maddow/watch/russian-lawyer-had-deep-ties-to-kremlin-emails-show-1221158979861.

10 Apuzzo et al.

11 Benjamin Weiser and Sharon LaFraniere, "Veselnitskaya, Russian in Trump Tower Meeting, Is Charged in Case That Shows Kremlin Ties," *New York Times*, January 8, 2019, https://www.nytimes.com/2019/01/08/nyregion/trump-tower-natalya-veselnitskaya-indictment.html.

12 Benjamin Weiser and Sharon LaFraniere, "Lawyer Who Was Said to Have Dirt on Clinton Had Closer Ties to Kremlin Than She Let On," *New York Times*, April 27, 2018, https://www.nytimes.com/2018/04/27/us/natalya-veselnitskaya-trump-tower-russian-prosecutor-general.html

.13 Robert Mueller III, *Report on the Investigation into Russian Interference in the 2016 Presidential Election*, Volume I of II, 122–123.

14 Office of Public Affairs, "Appointment of Special Counsel," Department of Justice, Wednesday, May 17, 2017, https://www.justice.gov/opa/pr/appointment-special-counsel.

15 George Papadopoulos, *Deep State Target: How I Got Caught in the Crosshairs of the Plot to Bring Down President Trump* (New York: Diversion Books, 2018), 167–168.

16 Ibid., 170.

17 Sara Carter, "Congress Wants Info: Former Top FBI Lawyer Being Investigated for Leaks," Saracarter.com, January 15, 2019, https://saraacarter.com/congress-wants-info-former-top-fbi-lawyer-being-investigated-for-leaks/.

18 Scott Shane, "Report Details Interactions Between F.B.I. and Dossier Author," *New York Times,* December 9, 2019, https://www.nytimes.com/2019/12/09/us/politics/fbi-steele-dossier.html.

CHAPTER 3

1 Central Intelligence Agency, "What We Do," last updated October 16, 2019, https://www.cia.gov/about-cia/todays-cia/what-we-do.

2   John O. Brennan (@johnbrennan), Twitter, July 16, 2018, 9:52 AM, https://twitter. com/johnbrennan/status/1018885971104985093?lang=en.

3   Charlie Savage, Adam Goldman, and Julian E. Barnes, "Justice Dept. Is Investigating C.I.A. Resistance to Sharing Russia Secrets," *New York Times,* February 13, 2020, https://www.nytimes.com/2020/02/13/us/politics/durham-cia-russia.html.

4   Office of the Director of National Intelligence, "Background to 'Assessing Russian Activities and Intentions in Recent US Elections': The Analytic Process and Cyber Incident Attribution," January 7, 2017, https://www.dni.gov/files/documents/ ICA_2017_01.pdf.

5   Admiral Michael Rogers, "Cybersecurity Threats and Defense Strategy," CSPAN, May 9, 2017, https://www.c-span.org/video/?428023-1/nsa-director-rogers-russia-poses-threat-congressional-elections.

6   Letter and attachment of footnote declassification from Richard Grenell, Acting Director, Office of Director of National Intelligence, to Senator Charles Grassley, chairman of Committee on Finance, and Senator Ron Johnson, chairman of the Committee on Homeland Security, April 15, 2020, https://www.grassley.senate. gov/sites/default/files/2020-04-15%20ODNI%20to%20CEG%20RHJ%20 %28FISA%20Footnote%20Declassification%29.pdf.

7   Ibid.

8   Ibid.

9   Luke Harding, Stephanie Kirchgaessner, and Nick Hopkins, "British Spies Were First to Spot Trump Team's Links with Russia," *The Guardian,* April 13, 2017, https://www.theguardian.com/uk-news/2017/apr/13/british-spies-first-to-spot-trump-team-links-russia.

10 Paul Wood, "Trump 'Compromising' Claims: How and Why Did We Get Here?" BBC, January 12, 2017, https://www.bbc.com/news/world-us-canada-38589427.

11 "Former C.I.A. Chief Tells of Concern Over Possible Russia Ties to Trump Campaign," *New York Times,* May 23, 2017, https://www.nytimes.com/2017/05/23/ us/politics/congress-testimony-john-brennan-russia-budget.html.

12 Simpson.

13 Eric Felten, "It Started with a Lie: Bruce Ohr's Linchpin Role in Collusion Narrative," RealClearPolitics, June 13, 2019, https://www.realclearpolitics.com/ articles/2019/06/13/it_started_with_a_lie_bruce_ohrs_linchpin_role_in_collu-sion_narrative.html.

14 Eric Felten, "Buried in IG Report: How an FBI Team in Rome Gave Steele Highly Guarded Secrets," RealClearInvestigations, February 14, 2020, https://www. realclearinvestigations.com/articles/2020/02/13/buried_in_ig_report_fbi_gave_ steele_highly_protected_secrets_122394.html.

15 Simpson.

16   Ellen Nakashima, "Russian Government Hackers Penetrated DNC, Stole Opposition Research on Trump," *Washington Post*, June 14, 2016, https://www.washingtonpost.com/world/national-security/russian-government-hackers-penetrated-dnc-stole-opposition-research-on-trump/2016/06/14/cf006cb4-316e-11e6-8ff7-7b6c1998b7a0_story.html.

17   Eric Lichtblau, "C.I.A. Had Evidence of Russian Effort to Help Trump Earlier Than Believed," *New York Times*, April 6, 2017, https://www.nytimes.com/2017/04/06/us/trump-russia-cia-john-brennan.html.

18   "Harry Reid's Letter to James Comey," *New York Times*, August 29, 2016, https://www.nytimes.com/interactive/2016/08/29/us/politics/document-Reid-Letter-to-Comey.html.

19   Lichtblau.

20   Office of the Inspector General, "Review of Four FISA Applications and Other Aspects of the FBI's Crossfire Hurricane Investigation," Department of Justice, December 2019 (revised), 179, https://www.justice.gov/storage/120919-examination.pdf.

21   Ibid.

22   Brett Samuels, "Ex-CIA Chief: Steele Dossier Played No Role in Intelligence Assessment on Russia's Election Interference," The Hill, February 4, 2018, https://thehill.com/homenews/sunday-talk-shows/372222-ex-cia-chief-steele-dossier-played-no-role-whatsoever-in.

23   Office of Inspector General, 180.

24   "Strzok-Page Texts (Redactions)," Fox News, May 28, 2019, https://www.scribd.com/document/411757906/Strzok-Page-texts.

25   Office of the Inspector General, v.

26   Ibid.

27   As I've reported elsewhere, FISA warrants come with a "one hop" rule, allowing probes of figures who come into the target's orbit.

28   Jeff Carlson, "Transcripts of Lisa Page's Closed-Door Testimonies Provide New Revelations in Spygate Scandal," *Epoch Times*, March 8, 2019, https://www.theepochtimes.com/transcripts-of-lisa-pages-closed-door-testimonies-provide-new-revelations_2763452.html.

29   Ibid.

CHAPTER 4

1   Office of the Press Secretary, "Presidential Policy Directive #41—United States Cyber Incident Coordination," July 26, 2016, https://obamawhitehouse.archives.gov/the-press-office/2016/07/26/presidential-policy-directive-united-states-cyber-incident.

2   Kim Zetter, "The Massive OPM Hack Actually Hit 21 Million People," *Wired*, July 9, 2015, https://www.wired.com/2015/07/massive-opm-hack-actually-affected-25-million/.

3   Ellen Nakashima, "Russian Government Hackers Penetrated DNC, Stole Opposition Research on Trump," *Washington Post*, June 14, 2016, https://www.washingtonpost.com/world/national-security/russian-government-hackers-penetrated-dnc-stole-opposition-research-on-trump/2016/06/14/cf006cb4-316e-11e6-8ff7-7b6c1998b7a0_story.html.

4   Department of Treasury, "Treasury Targets North Korea for Multiple Cyber-Attacks," press release, September 6, 2018, https://home.treasury.gov/news/press-releases/sm473.

5   The White House, Office of the Press Secretary, "Presidential Policy Directive—United States Cyber incident Coordination," press release, July 26, 2016, https://obamawhitehouse.archives.gov/the-press-office/2016/07/26/presidential-policy-directive-united-states-cyber-incident.

6   Paul Sperry, "Justice Dept. Watchdog Has Evidence Comey Probed Trump, on the Sly," RealClearInvestigations, July 22, 2019, https://www.realclearinvestigations.com/articles/2019/07/22/comey_under_scrutiny_for_own_inquiry_and_misleading_trump_119584.html.

7   Anthony Ferrante, "Exhibit 1: Expert Report of Anthony J. Ferrante FTI Consulting, Inc.," May 25, 2018, Aleksej Gubarev, XBT Holdings S.A., and Webzilla, Inc. v. Buzzfeed, Inc. and Ben Smith, 1:17-CV-60426-UU (Southern District of Florida, Miami Division), https://int.nyt.com/data/documenthelper/668-report-commissioned-by-buzzfee/b3e5dbe1c9086ae11ccc/optimized/full.pdf#page=1.

8   Jana Winter, "Former Senior FBI Official Is Leading BuzzFeed's Effort to Verify Trump Dossier," *Foreign Policy*, February 12, 2018, https://foreignpolicy.com/2018/02/12/former-senior-fbi-official-is-leading-buzzfeeds-effort-to-verify-trump-dossier/.

9   Matthew Rosenberg, "Tech Firm in Steele Dossier May Have Been Used by Russian Spies," *New York Times*, March 14, 2019, https://www.nytimes.com/2019/03/14/us/politics/gubarev-steele-dossier-trump-russia.html.

10 Daniel Chaitin, "Watchdog Files FOIA Lawsuit against FBI over James Comey's 'Spies' in the White House," *Washington Examiner*, September 5, 2019, https://www.washingtonexaminer.com/news/watchdog-files-foia-lawsuit-against-fbi-over-james-comeys-spies-in-the-white-house.

11 Sperry, RealClearInvestigations.

12 Tim Shipman, "Trump-Russia Dossier: Sex, Spies and Videotape," *Sunday Times*, January 26 2020, https://www.thetimes.co.uk/article/trump-russia-dossier-sex-spies-and-videotape-dtmzdg25q.

13 Arthur Snell, "Letters to the Editor: Trump-Russia Dossier Was Valid," *Sunday Times*, February 23, 2020.

14 Simpson, 83.

15 Chuck Grassley, "FBI Ignored Early Warnings That Debunked Anti-Trump Dossier Was Russian Disinformation," news release, April 10, 2020, https://www. grassley.senate.gov/news/news-releases/fbi-ignored-early-warnings-debunked-anti-trump-dossier-was-russian-disinformation.

16 John Solomon, "Russia Case Footnotes to Be Declassified, Exposing FBI Concerns about Steele Disinformation," Just the News, April 9, 2020, https:// justthenews.com/accountability/russia-and-ukraine-scandals/russia-case-footnotes-be-declassified-exposing-fbi.

CHAPTER 5

1 Charlie Savage, "Departing White House Counsel Held Powerful Sway," *New York Times*, April 6, 2014, https://www.nytimes.com/2014/04/07/us/politics/departing-white-house-counsel-held-powerful-sway.html.

2 Philip Rucker and Juliet Eilperin, "On IRS Issue, Senior White House Aides Were Focused on Shielding Obama," *Washington Post*, May 22, 2013, https://www. washingtonpost.com/politics/on-irs-issue-senior-white-house-aides-were-focused-on-shielding-obama/2013/05/22/9183902c-c228-11e2-914f-a7aba60512a7_story. html.

3 Ibid.

4 Carol D. Leonnig and David Nakamura, "Aides Knew of Possible White House Link to Cartagena, Colombia, Prostitution Scandal," *Washington Post*, October 8, 2014, https://www.washingtonpost.com/politics/aides-despite-denials-knew-of-white-house-tie-to-cartagena-prostitution-scandal/2014/10/08/5b98dc90-4e7e-11e4-aa5e-7153e466a02d_story.html.

5 Lauren Carroll, "Donald Trump's Syria Strike Looks a Lot Like Barack Obama's Plan, Despite What Rubio, Others Say," PolitiFact, April 12, 2017, https:// www.politifact.com/factchecks/2017/apr/12/marco-rubio/trumps-strikes-syria-look-lot-obamas-2013-proposal/.

6 Jacqueline Klimas, "Obama Launches 2,800 Strikes on Iraq, Syria without Congressional Approval," *Washington Times*, April 27, 2015, https://www.washingtontimes. com/news/2015/apr/27/congress-still-not-specifically-authorizing-islami/.

7 Sydney Powell, "All the President's Muses: Obama and Prosecutorial Misconduct," *Observer*, June 13, 2014, https://observer.com/2014/06/all-the-presidents-muses-obama-and-prosecutorial-misconduct/.

8 Senator Chuck Grassley, "Grassley, Graham Uncover 'Unusual Email' Sent by Susan Rice to Herself on President Trump's Inauguration Day," news release,

February 12, 2018, https://www.grassley.senate.gov/news/news-releases/grassley-graham-uncover-unusual-email-sent-susan-rice-herself-president-trump-s.

9 "Kathryn Ruemmler, Partner, Latham & Watkins LLP," Salzburg Global Seminar website, https://www.salzburgglobal.org/people.html?userID=37899&viewType=2.

10 Dania Akkad and Ian Cobain, "George Nader: How a Convicted Paedophile Became Key to an Emirati Hook-Up with Trump," Middle East Eye, July 5, 2019, https://www.middleeasteye.net/big-story/george-nader-how-convicted-paedophile-became-key-to-emirati-hook-trump.

11 Special Counsel Robert S. Mueller III, *Report on the Investigation into Russian Interference in the 2016 Presidential Election, March 2019*, p. 147, https://www.nytimes.com/interactive/2019/04/18/us/politics/mueller-report-document.html#g-page-147.

12 Ibid, 155.

13 Adam Entous, Greg Miller, Kevin Sieff, and Karen DeYoung, "Blackwater Founder Held Secret Seychelles Meeting to Establish Trump-Putin Back Channel," *Washington Post*, April 3, 2017, https://www.washingtonpost.com/world/national-security/blackwater-founder-held-secret-seychelles-meeting-to-establish-trump-putin-back-channel/2017/04/03/95908a08-1648-11e7-ada0-1489b735b3a3_story.html.

14 James Gordon Meek, "Mueller Witness Charged in Child Pornography Case," ABC News, June 3, 2019, https://abcnews.go.com/Politics/mueller-witness-charged-child-pornography-case/story?id=63461025.

15 Jerry Dunleavy, "Obama White House Lawyers Fight Carter Page's DNC Lawsuit by Defending 'Gist' of Steele Dossier," *Washington Examiner*, March 19, 2020, https://www.washingtonexaminer.com/news/obama-white-house-lawyers-fight-carter-pages-dnc-lawsuit-by-defending-gist-of-steele-dossier.

16 Ibid.

17 Office of the Inspector General, 172.

CHAPTER 6

1 Office of the Inspector General, vi.

2 Charlie Savage and Adam Goldman, "National Security Wiretap System Was Long Plagued by Risk of Errors and Omissions," *New York Times*, February 23, 2020, https://www.nytimes.com/2020/02/23/us/politics/fisa-surveillance-fbi.html.

3 Office of the Inspector General, 377.

4 Office the Inspector General, 52.

5 Office the Inspector General, 122.

6 Margot Cleveland, "Leak of Crossfire Hurricane Agent's Identity to the *NYT* Suggests More to Come," *The Federalist*, March 2, 2020, https://thefederalist.com/2020/03/02/leak-of-crossfire-hurricane-agents-identity-to-the-nyt-suggests-more-to-come/.

7   Inspector General Report, 98.

8   Office of the Inspector General, 98.

9   "U.S. Accuses 3 Russians of Spying," *New York Times,* April 4, 2017, https://www.nytimes.com/interactive/2017/04/04/world/europe/document-U-S-Accuses-Three-Russians-of-Spying.html.

10 Office of Inspector General, 55.

11 Office of the Inspector General, 377.

12 Ibid.

13 Office of the Inspector General, 314.

14 Leslie H. Gelb, "Reagan Aides Describe Operation to Gather Inside Data on Carter," *New York Times,* July 7, 1983, https://www.nytimes.com/1983/07/07/us/reagan-aides-describe-operation-to-gather-inside-data-on-carter.html.

15 Ibid, 315.

16 Ibid.

17 Ibid.

18 Margot Cleveland, "Exclusive Carter Page Interview Raises New Questions About 'Inaccuracy-Laden' IG Report," *The Federalist,* January 8, 2020, https://thefederalist.com/2020/01/08/exclusive-carter-page-interview-raises-new-questions-about-inaccuracy-laden-ig-report/.

19 Editorial Board, "When Carter Page Met Stefan Halper, *Wall Street Journal,* May 23, 2018, https://www.wsj.com/articles/when-carter-page-met-stefan-halper-1527029988.

20 Glenn Greenwald, "The FBI Informant Who Monitored the Trump Campaign, Stefan Halper, Oversaw a CIA Spying Operation in the 1980 Presidential Elections," *The Intercept,* May 2018, https://theintercept.com/2018/05/19/the-fbi-informant-who-monitored-the-trump-campaign-stefan-halper-oversaw-a-cia-spying-operation-in-the-1980-presidential-election/.

21 Margot Cleveland, "Grassley Letter Asks Whether Taxpayers Paid Russian Agent to Help Start the Collusion Hoax," *The Federalist,* January 24, 2020, https://thefederalist.com/2020/01/24/grassley-letter-asks-whether-taxpayers-paid-russian-agent-to-help-start-the-collusion-hoax/.

22 Cleveland, March 2.

CHAPTER 7

1   Max Boot, "Michael Flynn's Revelatory Report," *Commentary,* January 7, 2010, https://www.commentarymagazine.com/max-boot/michael-flynns-revelatory-report/.

2   Ibid.

3   James Kitfield, "How Mike Flynn Became America's Angriest General," *Politico*, October 16, 2016,https://www.politico.com/magazine/story/2016/10/how-mike-flynn-became-americas-angriest-general-214362.

4   Lieutenant General (Ret.) Michael T. Flynn and Michael Ledeen, *The Field of Fight: How We Can Win the Global War Against Radical Islam and Its Allies* (New York: St. Martin's Griffin, 2017), 131.

5   Kitfield.

6   Svetlana Lokhova v. Stefan A. Halper, 1:19-cv-632 (US District Court for the Eastern District of Virginia, Alexandria Division, May 23, 2019), https://www.courtlistener.com/recap/gov.uscourts.vaed.442627/gov.uscourts.vaed.442627.1.0_5.pdf.

7   Carol E. Lee, Rob Barry, Shane Harris, and Christopher S. Stewart, "Mike Flynn Didn't Report 2014 Interaction with Russian-British National," *Wall Street Journal*, March 18, 2017, https://www.wsj.com/articles/mike-flynn-didnt-report-2014-interaction-with-russian-british-national-1489809842.

8   Ibid.

9   FBI Washington Field Office, "Closing Communication," January 4, 2017, uploaded by *The Federalist*, https://www.scribd.com/document/459202552/CROSSFIRE-RAZOR-FBI-*Exonerated*-Flynn-But-Strzok-Reopened-Case-Against-Him.

10   Kitfield.

11   DHS Press Office, "Joint Statement from the Department of Homeland Security and Office of the Director of National Intelligence on Election Security," October 7, 2016, https://www.dhs.gov/news/2016/10/07/joint-statement-department-homeland-security-and-office-director-national.

12   "Logan Act, United States [1799]," *Encyclopedia Britannica*, https://www.britannica.com/event/Logan-Act.

13   Special Counsel Robert Mueller, "Statement of the Offense: United States of America v. Michael T. Flynn," 1:17-cr-00232-RC (US District Court for the District of Columbia, December 1, 2017), https://www.justice.gov/file/1015126/download.

14   Ibid.

15   Ryan Lizza, "Preserving the Russia Investigation: A Preview of Our Interview with Sally Yates," *The New Yorker*, March 16, 2017, https://www.newyorker.com/news/news-desk/preserving-the-russia-investigation-a-preview-of-our-interview-with-sally-yates?.

16   Andrew G. McCabe, *The Threat: How the FBI Protects America in the Age of Terror and Trump* (New York: St. Martin's Press, 2019),198–199.

17   Office of the Inspector General, 315.

18   Ibid.

19   David Ignatius, "Why Did Obama Dawdle on Russia's Hacking?" *Washington Post*, January 12, 2017, https://www.washingtonpost.com/opinions/why-did-obama-dawdle-on-russias-hacking/2017/01/12/75f878a0-d90c-11e6-9a36-1d296534b31e_story.html.

20 Ellen Nakashima and Greg Miller, "FBI Reviewed Flynn's Calls with Russian Ambassador but Found Nothing Illicit," *Washington Post*, January 23, 2017, https://www.washingtonpost.com/world/national-security/fbi-reviewed-flynns-calls-with-russian-ambassador-but-found-nothing-illicit/2017/01/23/aa83879a-e1ae-11e6-a547-5fb9411d332c_story.html.

21 Elizabeth Vaughn, "Little Noticed Whistleblower Story from August 2018 Involving ONA Director, Col. James Baker, Takes on Greater Significance in the Wake of Flynn Filing," RedState, October 27, 2019, https://www.redstate.com/elizabeth-vaughn/2019/10/27/little-noticed-whistleblower-story-august-2018-involving-ona-director-col.-james-baker-takes-greater-significance-wake-flynn-filing.

22 TheLastRefuge (@TheLastRefuge2), "Flynn Thread," Twitter, April 29, 2020, https://twitter.com/TheLastRefuge2/status/1255664023988772865.

23 Ibid.

24 Tobias Hoonhout, "Records Show Strzok Intervened When FBI Moved to Close Flynn Investigation Due to Lack of 'Derogatory Information,'" *National Review*, April 30, 2020, https://www.nationalreview.com/news/records-show-peter-strzok-intervened-when-fbi-moved-to-close-investigation-of-flynn-after-finding-no-derogatory-information/.

25 John Solomon, "FBI Found No 'Derogatory' Russia Evidence on Flynn, Planned to Close Case Before Leaders Intervened," Just the News, April 30, 2020, https://justthenews.com/accountability/russia-and-ukraine-scandals/fbi-found-no-derogatory-russia-evidence-flynn-planned.

26 E. W. Priestap, "Handwritten FBI Notes on Michael Flynn: 'Get Him Fired,'" *The Federalist*, April 29, 2020, https://www.scribd.com/document/459056127/Handwritten-FBI-Notes-On-Michael-Flynn-Get-Him-Fired#from_embed.

27 "Government's Motion to Dismiss the Criminal Information against the Defendant Michael T. Flynn, Exhibit 4: Interview of Sally Yates" (United States District Court for the District of Columbia, May 7, 2020), https://int.nyt.com/data/documenthelper/6936-michael-flynn-motion-to-dismiss/fa06f5e13a0ec71843b6/optimized/full.pdf.

28 Ibid.

29 Office of the Director of National Intelligence, "Background to 'Assessing Russian Activities and Intentions in Recent US Elections': The Analytic Process and Cyber Incident Attribution," January 7, 2017, https://www.dni.gov/files/documents/ICA_2017_01.pdf.

30 Office of the Inspector General, 180.

31 Sydney Powell, "Motion to Compel the Production of Brady Material and for an Order to Show Cause" (US District Court for the District of Columbia, August 30, 2019), https://www.scribd.com/document/425453884/DCD-Flynn-Motion-to-Compel.

32   Emmet G. Sullivan, "Order: Criminal No. 17-232-01" (US District Court for the District of Columbia, February 16, 2018), https://www.courtlistener.com/recap/gov.uscourts.dcd.191592/gov.uscourts.dcd.191592.20.0.pdf.

33   Alex Pappas, "Comey Admits Decision to Send FBI Agents to Interview Flynn Was not Standard," Fox News, December 13, 2018, https://www.foxnews.com/politics/comey-admits-decision-to-send-fbi-agents-to-interview-mike-flynn-was-not-standard.

34   Peter Strzok, "302 of Michael Flynn," FBI, February 15, 2017, https://www.documentcloud.org/documents/5633496-181217-Flynn-302.htmPl.

35   Ibid.

36   Ibid.

37   FBI, "DAD: Peter P. Strzok Interview," Attachment B in Government's Reply to Defendant's Memorandum in Aid of Sentencing," December 18, 2018, https://assets.documentcloud.org/documents/5628484/Show-Temp.pdf.

38   Svetlana Lokhova.

39   Timothy Shea, "Government's Motion to Dismiss the Criminal Information against the Defendant Michael T. Flynn," (US District Court for the District of Columbia, May 7, 2020), https://int.nyt.com/data/documenthelper/6936-michael-flynn-motion-to-dismiss/fa06f5e13a0ec71843b6/optimized/full.pdf.

40   Jeff Jensen, "Statement on Flynn Case," @kerrikupecDOJ, May 7, 2020, https://twitter.com/KerriKupecDOJ/status/1258476453894795276.

41   Jeff Mordock, "Judge's Move Opens Door to Appeal of Decision Ordering Dismissal of Flynn Case," *Washington Times*, June 24, 2020,https://www.washingtontimes.com/news/2020/jun/24/judge-emmett-sullivan-may-appeal-michael-flynn-dis.

42   United States v. Michael Flynn,1:17-cr-00232-RC, https://www.justice.gov/file/1015126/download.

43   Peter Strzok.

44   Brandon L. Van Grack, "Government's Memorandum in Aid of Sentencing" (US District Court for the District of Columbia, December 18, 2018), https://www.courtlistener.com/recap/gov.uscourts.dcd.191592/gov.uscourts.dcd.191592.46.0_2.pdf.

CHAPTER 8

1   Robert Spalding III, *Stealth War: How China Took Over While America's Elite Slept,* (New York: Portfolio, 2019), 124.

2   "Declassified Memorandum of Telephone Conversation—Subject: Telephone Conversation with President Zelensky of Ukraine; Participants: President Zelensky, July 25, 2019," whitehouse.gov, https://www.whitehouse.gov/wp-content/uploads/2019/09/Unclassified09.2019.pdf.

3   Anonymous letter to Richard Burr, chairman of the US Senate Select Committee on Intelligence, and Adam Schiff, chairman of the US House Permanent Select Committee on Intelligence, from the Trump-Ukraine whistleblower, August 12, 2019, https:// intelligence.house.gov/uploadedfiles/20190812_-_whistleblower_complaint_ unclass.pdf.

4   Letter from Michael K. Atkinson, inspector general of Intelligence Committee, to Joseph Maguire, acting director of Intelligence Community, August 26, 2019, https://intelligence.house.gov/uploadedfiles/20190826_-_icig_letter_to_acting_ dni_unclass.pdf.

5   Paul Sperry, "The Beltway's 'Whistleblower' Furor Obsesses Over One Name," RealClearInvestigations, October 30, 2019, https://www.realclearinvestigations.com/ articles/2019/10/30/whistleblower_exposed_close_to_biden_brennan_dnc_oppo_ researcher_120996.html.

6   Sperry.

7   Daniel Chaitin and Jerry Dunleavy, "John McCain Associate Behind Dossier Leak Urged BuzzFeed to Retract Its Story: 'You Are Gonna Get People Killed!'" Washington Examiner, March 14, 2019, https://www.washingtonexaminer.com/news/ john-mccain-associate-behind-dossier-leak-urged-buzzfeed-to-retract-its-story-you-are-gonna-get-people-killed.

8   Department of Justice, search results of Foreign Agents Registration Act on Query "Pinchuk," https://search.justice.gov/search?query=pinchuk&op=Search& affiliate=justice_fara.

9   Polina Ivanova, Maria Tsvetkova, Ilya Zhegulev, and Luke Baker, "What Hunter Biden Did on the Board of Ukrainian Energy Company Burisma," Reuters, October 18, 2019, https://www.reuters.com/article/us-hunter-biden-ukraine/ what-hunter-biden-did-on-the-board-of-ukrainian-energy-company-burisma-idUSKBN1WX1P7.

10 Eric J. Friedman, "Registration Statement Pursuant to the Foreign Agents Registration Act of 1938, as Amended," January 18, 2019, https://efile.fara.gov/ docs/6617-Registration-Statement-20190118-1.pdf.

11 Mike McIntire, "Manafort Was in Debt to Pro-Russia Interests, Cyprus Records Show," New York Times, July 19, 2017, https://www.nytimes.com/2017/07/19/us/ politics/paul-manafort-russia-trump.html.

12 David Holmes, "Deposition of David Holmes," Permanent Select Committee on Intelligence, Joint with the Committee on Oversight And Reform and the Committee on Foreign Affairs, US House of Representatives, November 15, 2019, 24, https://assets.documentcloud.org/documents/6552622/Holmes-Final-Version-Redacted.pdf.

13 Ibid., 25.

14 Greg Miller and Greg Jaffe, "In Aftermath of Ukraine Crisis, a Climate of Mistrust and Threats," *Washington Post*, December 25, 2019, https://www.washingtonpost.com/national-security/in-aftermath-of-ukraine-crisis-a-climate-of-mistrust-and-threats/2019/12/24/03831e3e-2359-11ea-a153-dce4b94e4249_story.html.

15 John Solomon, "FBI's Steele Story Falls Apart: False Intel and Media Contacts Were Flagged Before FISA," The Hill, May 9, 2019, https://thehill.com/opinion/white-house/442944-fbis-steele-story-falls-apart-false-intel-and-media-contacts-were-flagged.

16 Citizens United v. State FOIA (New DOS Kavalec Emails), January 22, 2020, http://www.citizensunited.org/latest-updates.aspx?article=11717.

17 Jeffery Toobin, "Adam Schiff's Plans to Obliterate Trump's Red Line," *The New Yorker*, December 14, 2018, https://www.newyorker.com/magazine/2018/12/24/adam-schiffs-plans-to-obliterate-trumps-red-line.

18 Ibid.

19 Betsy McCaughey, "Getting the Goods on Schiff," RealClearPolitics, January 2, 2020, https://www.realclearpolitics.com/articles/2020/01/02/getting_the_goods_on_schiff_142062.html.

20 Julian E. Barnes, Michael S. Schmidt, and Matthew Rosenberg, "Schiff Got Early Account of Accusations as Whistle-Blower's Concerns Grew," *New York Times*, October 2, 2019, https://www.nytimes.com/2019/10/02/us/politics/adam-schiff-whistleblower.html.

21 Mary McCord, "State of the Rule of Law in the U.S.: Where Are We Now and What Is to Come?," Brookings Institute, October 3, 2018, https://www.brookings.edu/wp-content/uploads/2018/10/gs_20181003_rule_of_law_transcript.pdf.

22 "Michael Atkinson: Trump Fires Intelligence Chief Involved in Impeachment," BBC News, April 4, 2020, https://www.bbc.com/news/world-us-canada-52164706.

23 Margot Cleveland, "Did the Inspector General's Office Help the 'Whistleblower' Try to Frame Trump?" *The Federalist*, September 30, 2019, https://thefederalist.com/2019/09/30/did-the-inspector-generals-office-help-the-whistleblower-try-to-frame-trump/.

24 Atkinson.

25 Letter from Michael Atkinson, inspector general of Intelligence Community, to Adam Schiff, chairman, US House Permanent Select Committee on Intelligence, and Devin Nunes, ranking member, US House Permanent Select Committee on Intelligence, regarding Maguire's failure to notify Congress, September 9, 2019, https://www.scribd.com/document/426585488/Sept-9-letter-from-Intel-Inspector-General-to-House-Intelligence-on-whistleblower-complaint#from_embed.

26 Marty Johnson and J. Edward Moreno, "Barr Said Firing Inspector General Was 'Right Thing,'" The Hill, April 10, 2020, https://thehill.com/homenews/administration/492162-barr-says-trump-firing-inspector-general-was-right-thing.

27   Julian E. Barnes, Michael S. Schmidt, and Matthew Rosenberg, "Schiff Got Early Account of Accusations as Whistle-Blower's Concerns Grew," *New York Times*, October 2, 2019, https://www.nytimes.com/2019/10/02/us/politics/adam-schiff-whistleblower.html.

28   Letter from Adam Schiff, chairman, US House Permanent Select Committee on Intelligence, to acting director of National Intelligence Joseph Maguire, about forwarding whistleblower complaint, September 10, 2019, https://intelligence.house.gov/uploadedfiles/20190910_-_chm_schiff_letter_to_acting_dni_maguire.pdf.

CHAPTER 9

1   Tony Romm, "Americans Have Filed More Than 40 Million Jobless Claims in Past 10 Weeks," *Washington Post*, May 28, 2020, https://www.washingtonpost.com/business/2020/05/28/unemployment-claims-coronavirus/.

2   Shengjie Lai, Nick W. Ruktanonchai, Liangcai Zhou, et al., *"Effect of Non-Pharmaceutical Interventions for Containing the COVID-19 Outbreak in China,"* medRXiv, March 9, 2020, https://www.medrxiv.org/content/10.1101/2020.03.03.20029843v3?mod=article_inline.

3   Chaolin Huang, Yeming Wang, Xingwang Li, et al., "Clinical Features of Patients Infected with 2019 Novel Coronavirus in Wuhan, China," *The Lancet*, January 24, 2020, https://www.thelancet.com/journals/lancet/article/PIIS0140-6736(20)30183-5/fulltext#bib35.

4   James T. Areddy, "China Bat Expert Says Her Wuhan Lab Wasn't Source of New Coronavirus," *Wall Street Journal*, April 21, 2020, https://www.wsj.com/articles/chinas-bats-expert-says-her-wuhan-lab-wasnt-source-of-new-coronavirus-11587463204.

5   Ken Dilanian, Ruaridh Arrow, Courtney Kube, et al., "Report Says Cellphone Data Suggests October Shutdown at Wuhan Lab, but Experts Are Skeptical," NBC News, May 8, 2020, https://www.nbcnews.com/politics/national-security/report-says-cellphone-data-suggests-october-shutdown-wuhan-lab-experts-n1202716.

6   Zhuang Pinghui, "China Confirms Unauthorised Labs Were Told to Destroy Early Coronavirus Samples," *South China Morning Post*, May 15, 2020, https://www.scmp.com/news/china/society/article/3084635/china-confirms-unauthorised-labs-were-told-destroy-early.

7   Spalding, xi-xii.

8   Central Committee of the Communist Party of China's General Office, "Document 9: Communiqué on the Current State of the Ideological Sphere," ChinaFile translation, November 8, 2013, https://www.chinafile.com/document-9-chinafile-translation.

9   Spalding, 199.

10   Joe Parkinson, Nicholas Bariyo, and Josh Chin, "Huawei Technicians Helped African Governments Spy on Political Opponents," *Wall Street Journal,* August 15, 2019, https://www.wsj.com/articles/huawei-technicians-helped-african-governments-spy-on-political-opponents-11565793017.

11   Xinhua News Agency, "'Made in China 2025' Plan Unveiled," *China Daily,* updated May 19, 2015, https://www.chinadaily.com.cn/bizchina/2015-05/19/content_20760528.htm.

12   Spalding, 178.

13   Office of the United States Trade Representative, "Findings of the Investigation into China's Acts, Policies, and Practices Related to Technology Transfer, Intellectual Property, and Innovation Under Section 301 of the Trade Act of 1974," March 22, 2018, https://ustr.gov/sites/default/files/Section%20301%20FINAL.PDF.

14   "A Quick Guide to the US-China Trade War," BBC News, January 16, 2020, https://www.bbc.com/news/business-45899310.

15   Spalding, 62.

16   Felicia Sonmez, "Biden Says China Is 'Not Competition for US,' Prompting Pushback from Both Parties," *Washington Post,* May 2, 2019, https://www.washingtonpost.com/politics/biden-says-china-is-not-competition-for-us-prompting-pushback-from-republicans/2019/05/01/4ae4e738-6c68-11e9-a66d-a82d3f3d96d5_story.html.

17   Yong Xiong, Hande Atay Alam, and Nectar Gan, "Wuhan Hospital Announces Death of Whistleblower Doctor Li Wenlian," CNN, February 7, 2020, https://www.cnn.com/2020/02/06/asia/li-wenliang-coronavirus-whistleblower-doctor-dies-intl/index.html.

18   Thomas Ricker, "The US, Like China, Has About One Surveillance Camera for Every Four People, Says Report," The Verge, December, 9, 2019, https://www.theverge.com/2019/12/9/21002515/surveillance-cameras-globally-us-china-amount-citizens.

19   Taiwan Centers for Disease Control, "The Facts Regarding Taiwan's Email to Alert WHO to Possible Danger of COVID-19," May 11, 2020, https://www.cdc.gov.tw/En/Bulletin/Detail/PAD-lbwDHeN_bLa-viBOuw?typeid=158.

20   David Lin, "Letters to the Editor: Taiwan's response to covid-19," *The Economist,* March 26, https://www.economist.com/taxonomy/term/27/518697?page=41.

21   Ibid.

22   World Health Organization (@WHO), "…no clear evidence of human to human transmission," Twitter, January 14, 2020, 4:18 AM, https://twitter.com/WHO/status/1217043229427761152.

23   World Health Organization, "WHO Timeline—COVID-19," April 27, 2020, https://www.who.int/news-room/detail/27-04-2020-who-timeline---covid-19.

24 Jamie Ducharme, "The World Health Organization's Maria Van Kerkhove on Balancing Science, Public Relations and Politics," *Time*, April 27, 2020, https://time.com/5827383/maria-van-kerkhove-world-health-organization/.

25 Brett D. Schaefer, "How the U.S. Should Address Rising Chinese Influence at the United Nations," Heritage Foundation, August 20, 2019, https://www.heritage.org/sites/default/files/2019-08/BG3431_0.pdf.

26 Hinnerk Feldwisch-Drentrup, "How WHO Became China's Coronavirus Accomplice," *Foreign Policy*, April 2, 2020, https://foreignpolicy.com/2020/04/02/china-coronavirus-who-health-soft-power/.

27 Donald G. McNeil Jr., "Candidate to Lead the W.H.O. Accused of Covering Up Epidemics," *New York Times*, May 13, 2017, https://www.nytimes.com/2017/05/13/health/candidate-who-director-general-ethiopia-cholera-outbreaks.html.

28 Ibid.

29 Lanhee J. Chen, "Lost in Beijing: The Story of the WHO," *Wall Street Journal*, April 8, 2020, https://www.wsj.com/articles/lost-in-beijing-the-story-of-the-who-11586365090.

30 Ibid.

31 Sebastian Horn, Carmen Reinhart, and Christoph Trebesch, "China's Overseas Lending," Kiel Institute, April 16, 2020, https://www.ifw-kiel.de/fileadmin/Dateiverwaltung/IfW-Publications/Christoph_Trebesch/KWP_2132.pdf.

32 Fan Wei, Yang Cheng, and Cui Meng, "Ringing the Alarm: Wuhan Doctor Awarded for Making First Warning of Novel Disease Before Outbreak," *Global Times*, February 6, 2020, https://www.globaltimes.cn/content/1178756.shtml.

33 Sandip Sen, "How China Locked Down Internally for COVID-19, but Pushed Foreign Travel," *Economic Times*, April 30, 2020, https://economictimes.indiatimes.com/blogs/Whathappensif/how-china-locked-down-internally-for-covid-19-but-pushed-foreign-travel/.

34 WHO, "Statement on the Second Meeting of the International Health Regulations (2005) Emergency Committee Regarding the Outbreak of Novel Coronavirus (2019-nCoV)," January 30, 2020, https://www.who.int/news-room/detail/30-01-2020-statement-on-the-second-meeting-of-the-international-health-regulations-(2005)-emergency-committee-regarding-the-outbreak-of-novel-coronavirus-(2019-ncov).

35 Donald Trump, "Proclamation on Suspension of Entry as Immigrants and Nonimmigrants of Persons Who Pose a Risk of Transmitting 2019 Novel Coronavirus," January 31, 2020, whitehouse.gov, https://www.whitehouse.gov/presidential-actions/proclamation-suspension-entry-immigrants-nonimmigrants-persons-pose-risk-transmitting-2019-novel-coronavirus/.

36 Sen.

37 Steve Eder, Henry Fountain, Michael H. Keller, et al., "430,000 People Have Traveled from China to U.S. Since Coronavirus Surfaced," *New York Times,* April 4, 2020, https://www.nytimes.com/2020/04/04/us/coronavirus-china-travel-restrictions.html.

38 Yong-Zhen Zhang and Edward C. Holmes, "A Genomic Perspective on the Origin and Emergence of SARS-CoV-2," *Cell,* vol. 181, April 16, 2020, https://www.cell.com/cell/pdf/S0092-8674(20)30328-7.pdf.

39 Donald J. Trump (@realDonaldTrump), copy of letter from Trump to Director-General Tedros, May 18, 2020, Twitter, May 18, 2020, 8:55 PM, https://twitter.com/realDonaldTrump/status/1262577580718395393/photo/1.

CHAPTER 10

1 Office of the Inspector General, "A Report of Certain Allegations Relating to Former FBI Deputy Director Andrew McCabe," February, 2018,https://static01.nyt.com/files/2018/us/politics/20180413a-doj-oig-mccabe-report.pdf.

2 J. P. Cooney and Molly Gaston, "Re: Andrew McCabe," U.S. Department of Justice, District of Columbia, February 14, 2020, https://www.politico.com/f/?id=00000170-44c0-dfac-a9fb-cfdabde80000.